Parodies of the Fall

PARODIES OF THE FALL

THOMAS GRISSOM

SUNSTONE
PRESS

SANTA FE

Sunstone books may be purchased for educational, business, or sales promotional use.
For information please write: Special Markets Department, Sunstone Press,
P.O. Box 2321, Santa Fe, New Mexico 87504-2321.

Book and cover design › R. Ahl
Printed on acid-free paper
∞

Library of Congress Cataloging-in-Publication Data

Names: Grissom, Thomas, 1940- author.
Title: Parodies of the fall : a novel / by Thomas Grissom.
Description: Santa Fe, New Mexico : Sunstone Press, [2020] | Includes
    reader's guide. | Summary: "What unfolds in the strange story revealed
    by the narrator are the moral dilemmas faced by the human consciousness
    in the twenty-first century, leaving the reader to ponder whether
    anything is resolved"-- Provided by publisher.
Identifiers: LCCN 2020019636 | ISBN 9781632933027 (paperback) | ISBN
    9781611395990 (epub)
Subjects: LCGFT: Novels. | Parodies (Literature)
Classification: LCC PS3607.R577 P37 2020 | DDC 813/.6--dc23
LC record available at https://lccn.loc.gov/2020019636

WWW.SUNSTONEPRESS.COM
SUNSTONE PRESS / POST OFFICE BOX 2321 / SANTA FE, NM 87504-2321 /USA
(505) 988-4418 / FAX (505) 988-1025

To keep a promise to Studs Terkel

Parody? There is a narrow distinction between literature and parody, my friend. In a work that aims at seriousness, it can be a kindness to the reader to err on the side of comedy.

I walked in a desert.
And I cried,
"Ah, God, take me from this place!"
A voice said, "It is no desert."
I cried, "Well, but—
The sand, the heat, the vacant horizon."
A voice said, "It is no desert."
                —Stephen Crane

PREFACE

This is a story about finding meaning in a life lived in constant peril, against a backdrop of some vague, undisclosed but ominous and omnipresent threat. The central question posed by the novel is how to live "life as it should be," faced with the stark reality of "life as it is." In his search for an answer, the narrator tells his personal story nightly to a curious and eager companion, whose responses we can only infer from the narrator's comments, and who quickly becomes a silent surrogate for the reader. Chapter by chapter, bit by bit, the narrator reveals the gradual evolution of the human consciousness and mature voice that we find in his narrative. The conclusions he draws from the events that have shaped his life are unexpectedly ironic and often starkly counter to the more naïve expectations of his companion—and the reader. And yet, in spite of all the seeming contradictions, the narrator's answer to the riddle of "life as it should be," slowly emerges from his revealing insights into "life as it is." The narrator insists throughout that he has not contradicted himself, even making that assertion the concluding point of his narrative, for the reader to ponder in finding meaning in the story.

1

Pardon? What do you ask? Why yes, of course you may join me. In fact, please do. No, no, I insist. I was not hesitating, I assure you; only it is difficult to hear amidst this clamor, and I did not wish to appear presumptuous.

In truth, you are heartily welcome. It is at times like these that one most craves company, and at last learns to appreciate and enjoy it. I can see by your face that you agree.

Besides, what choice do you have? It seems that my little corner of this darkness is the only one not occupied. All these others are eager to be here, no doubt—they would not miss it for anything—but only if they don't have to think too much. Although they tolerate me, they grow tired of my chatter; they are annoyed by it, like a ringing in the ears that comes and goes, or a conversation overheard, too faint to be properly understood. Every place has its eccentrics, and here they are content to accord me that role.

Still, I don't feel estranged. We are all part of this now, and I can see that you at least understand. Clearly, you are not like them. You have honest eyes and a steady gaze. First, one forgets how to see, and then finally no longer even bothers to look. It is reassuring that there are still some who insist on what others will not face, but cannot deny.

Please, do not be offended. Here, we will order drinks: request whatever it is you are drinking. He will return with them promptly. This one knows me well and will not keep us waiting. We have often sat and talked about these same matters—before he too no longer wished to think about it any more. Since then I have brought him much business and many gratuities. Now, money is what he thinks about. Let me assure you it is not over-familiarity or lack of regard that makes me presume to take you into my confidence. It is only that I can see you are different.

And in a world of sameness, any difference is a welcome solace.

Ah, but you smile. I am not surprised that I amuse you. After all, who anymore would expect to encounter seriousness, especially in this place, where people come mainly to escape? It is the same all over. Everyone seeks to escape; and when escape is the only option remaining, then all are trapped together. By now they have had their noses rubbed in it once too often. Who can fault them for turning away when they have the chance? Most have long since come to the realization that there are no answers anyway. Why keep on searching when one no longer knows what the dispute is all about? We are not creatures of futility; not by choice at least. Folly perhaps, but not futility. We got here by demanding certainty, indeed by inventing it when we couldn't find it, and pretending at every turn. And it has always worked before. The path to where we are was walked in the footsteps of so many others, how is it possible that we could have lost our way?

Isn't that closer to the truth than not? This place, my friend, in spite of appearances, is actually a denial of futility. That is what brings us here, what brought me here in the beginning; what brings each of them back, night after night, every escape rooted in the illusion of some certainty: This one when all others fail! Our souls for it! We would gladly—even eagerly!—strike a Faustian bargain in the prospect. For it is written: "What can it profit a man to save his own soul if in so doing he shall lose the meaning of life?", etc., etc.

Then you caught the point of my little mockery? An innocent joke, nothing more. I meant no harm by it, I assure you. You know the passage I had in mind? Yes, I thought you might. One senses that you are a person of some refinement, not at all like the last boor who tried to occupy that chair. Yes; yes, I like that: a *chair*. Not merely a seat—that is to say, a place—but a *position* of rank and status. You and I occupy the only *chairs* in this establishment. All the others are seats and their occupants simply spectators. But we, my friend, we occupy chairs, endowed ones at that. Handsomely endowed, I might add, by the substantial sums all of your predecessors have paid into the coffers of this esteemed institution.

How shall we designate them? May I suggest this: *That* one shall be the Distinguished Chair of the Philosophy of Life as It Should Be; *this* one the Endowed Chair of the Philosophy of Life as It Is. We are agreed then? Good. Now that is settled, we may continue. Just in time: here are our drinks. No, it is not necessary, my friend; but certainly, if you prefer; and very generous of you too. We shall just regard it as the first installment on your share of the endowment.

A toast then. Here's to your long and illustrious tenure as the Distinguished Professor of Life as It Should Be. However, let me warn you. Though this chair has been easy enough to hold on to, no one has yet managed to occupy that one for any length. Your predecessors have not been a very distinguished lot. The last quit in disgust after less time than you have held the position. Quite a few of them drank excessively. None could confront life as it is. They were not much better either at deciding how it should be, though each believed it a simple enough task at the outset. I am afraid I incensed them with my prattle. You see, I had the easier position to uphold. They soon became frustrated by having to argue hypothetically in support of first this position and then that one, when all the evidence was on my side.

And I didn't help matters much; I developed little respect for them. Instead of approaching this exchange with the proper attitude, as what life is all about, they treated it with contempt as another of their foolish contests, to be won or lost, as if life has any winners. They were still hung up on the need for reasons and wanted to indulge and gratify themselves by pointing fingers and fixing blame. It was convenient enough to blame me, so I inevitably became the object of their scorn. One, like Meletus, accused me of always making the lesser appear the greater, and of making the weaker argument defeat the stronger. You have read Plato? You restore my faith, sir; we will get along famously. I would gladly play Anytus to your Socrates.

An apology? Why, you confound me, my friend. For what? Oh, that. No, it is truly uncalled for. Let's just say that I *meant* to amuse you. Without a sense of humor we are nothing. At times it seems like all we have left, and these days anyone can be too serious. I count it my good fortune, and another indication of your sensitive and generous nature, that you were so easily amused.

Yet it was my manner of speaking, was it not, that first put you off balance? I am not the least surprised. I have come to expect it. Do you recall my remark about searching for solace in a featureless landscape? You were anticipating instead the babble we hear all around us. I, on the other hand, was speaking in a fashion I save for such occasions. It is a manner of speaking reserved for the truth.

But you are quite right to be skeptical: the mark of a discerning nature. Of what possible concern are style and erudition to the truth, you ask? In a matter where substance is of the essence, count it if you will a gesture of respect and sincerity, a fine distinction of how best to proceed. Drowned out by the vulgar chorus, the ear is attuned to that difference, however slight, that heralds some new direction; perhaps a return to the old verities of the past, or some new discovery—or merely the respect that accords either the possibility of attainment. Arrived at with a certain charm and grace, we are on the one hand more confident that it *is* the truth, and on the other more inclined to accept it when it goes counter to our prejudices. We expect the truth to have a dignified bearing, even when it wears a stern countenance. The truth of our present circumstances is hard enough to accept in any guise. Spoken too harshly, it merely falls on deaf ears.

Isn't the reason, my friend, that we confuse truth with beauty, where, by the latter, what we have in mind is whatever is *pleasant*? These new truths are not pleasant. They sting, and they carry the stench of death. Yes, you are quite right, there is really nothing new about them. They are the same reality we have always faced: the senseless specter of death; the unfathomable significance of it; the abject meaninglessness; the mystery—no, I'll not say mystery, for that almost implies that there might be some meaning—its utter futility. What is the term which has come to symbolize our own encounter? Absurdity? Yes—its absurdity, the cruelest joke of all: given a consciousness that we may contemplate our own insignificance, our total lack of meaning.

Before it has always been possible to hide, to take refuge in some intellectual or emotional hoax. But now we are facing the inevitable. Every refuge has its limits and they are about to be sorely tested. One can entertain almost any fantasy at a distance, when it is merely a pleasant diversion; but not if one's entire being depends upon it. Then the matter of judgment becomes important. We demand certainty; and if we can't be sure of it then we insist on at least choosing the best odds. And not every choice appears equally attractive. At this moment it is safe to say that none of them are very reassuring.

Look around you. See their faces? What at some other time might pass for laughter masks a nervous apprehension: the unsettling conviction that this at long last *is* the truth. And it is a bitter pill to swallow, a blow to our self-esteem to realize that we are no different after all, merely a more complex and sophisticated dinosaur, but a dinosaur nevertheless, making the same soon-to-be-fossilized footprints, to give way ultimately to something else. Not something better, for that would only be confusing truth with hope, but merely something else, something different.

There is no rush to commit the definitive act, to take the ultimate way out. There is always the gamble that one is deceived, even after the odds are overwhelming. And hope is distinct from the truth. Truth is whatever will be. Hope is the sum of all the possibilities. That, my friend, is where we are different, distinct from the dinosaur, distinct even from ourselves when our circumstances no longer offer any reason for hope. When all that is apparent is an inner hopelessness, there is still *hope*; it is the defining characteristic of our existence, what it means to be uniquely human. It comes with the consciousness, the absurdity. It is at the same time the cause *and* the one thing that redeems it, that can make it bearable.

No, they don't surrender. Hope is more enduring than the truth; we will give it up last. It just may be what gets us through this. And if not it will keep us obeying whatever biological urge gave rise to it, for as long as whatever blind purpose it serves requires, for whatever unknown and unknowable destiny is ours; and still there will be *hope*. We are its undeniable reality, its existence proof, the very expression of it. To be rid of it will require the death of the last solitary human, like the last passenger pigeon, caged and alone at the end, staring blankly but still wondering, always wondering. I tell you, my friend, it is magnificent! After that, who knows? What happened once may have been no accident. You see, there is even a way for hope to transcend the inevitable. We can set it in motion now and it will last forever. As long as there is no certainty there will always be hope.

And who would have it any different? Certainly not them. They would have certainty with their hope but only if it leads to the desired conclusion. Otherwise, hope will triumph; it is everything.

They would not be here otherwise. This one is no different from any other escape, and more honest at that. Besides, here one can maintain the degree of detachment so vital to good judgment—that is to say, to recognizing the truth, to keeping truth and hope and certainty in the proper balance. After all, we define them; we must make the choices. If we can be assured of no other meaning outside ourselves then the burden is on us. No truth without certainty; and nothing at all without hope.

Ah, but it is *not* futile, my friend; it is everything. Look around you again. Did you not notice the name of this establishment? There, over the stage. Yes, that's it: *Act IV*, a theatrical flourish. The present owner gave it that name shortly after he acquired it. Before that it was the *Last Chance Saloon*. Not very original, to be sure. An artifact of an adventuresome frontier spirit, a holdover from a bygone era but sincere and authentic nevertheless. For many down through the years it probably was their last chance, or their last best hope. In those days there was gambling. Now all is a gamble and one does not need the click of the dice to be reminded. The new proprietor has a passion for the theater, especially for the great tragedies of antiquity and those of the Elizabethan stage and for those deeply disturbing dramas of our own time. Note, however, that the marquee and the insignia prominently display both masks: the smiling face of comedy, as well as that of tragedy. Are they not inseparable, almost indistinguishable? There can be no acceptance of the one without acknowledgment of the other.

The owner had that in mind when he chose. Apparently he felt the previous name was too explicit, an affront to the complexity of our situation, a denial of its possibilities. We must maintain our suppleness. Like those dramas of which he is so fond. It is undeniably late in the play but still it is not over. Even if the ending is known it is not without its own possibilities. Euripides proclaimed according to the formula, but he was still Euripides and that made the difference. And life, like art, has no set pattern, no unalterable form. It is created anew each moment out of all the infinite possibilities.

But of course I truly believe it, my friend; we all do. Why else would we persist? So what if it is late in the fourth act? A play can have any length, and this one, we fervently hope, will go on forever in spite of what we see swirling around us. It is being written and staged and directed all at the same time. Each moment the script is being refined, the actors staying right on cue, improvising and filling in as necessary, stage directions being whispered from the wings. And the play goes on.

But what about the truth, you ask? Yes, what of it? The truth of the matter may be otherwise. We must always keep it in mind. And yet the drama unfolds as it will. Here there can be no certainty except that which we are willing to believe in. For some, the truth demands finality, and they imagine one ending. Others conceive a different script and a play with always one more act. Even a tragedy has more than one truth. There is the truth of its tragic destiny; but there is also the truth of the hope it gives rise to. Who is to say which is the more compelling? You may write more than one ending but you must choose.

What do I think is the truth? The truth about what, my friend? Our fate? I see: the true "philosophy of life as it is," from the one who currently occupies the endowed chair of that position, is that it? So you took my little jest seriously. I had hoped you might. I find it most gratifying that you did not just dismiss it as a meaningless joke. For I, my friend, am most serious. I have spent my entire existence experiencing life as it is. In truth, if I may say so, it is all that I know—all that any of us can know, that we are ever permitted to know.

Perhaps, though, we are missing a point here. In light of our present circumstances is it not more urgent that we should discuss instead the "philosophy of life as it should be"? I would of course be most willing, even eager, to develop the dialectic under your direction. Perhaps between the two of us, with a few drinks, we can sever the Gordian knot of this present stranglehold. If not, well at least we will have spent the time as one should. And in so doing we may even put philosophy back on center stage with the actors, where it should be. In due course, you say? At the proper time. But first we must examine things as they are, to find the truth of it. I quite agree. Before one can build a better anything it is necessary to understand the pieces with which we have to work.

It seems that my confidence in your discerning nature is rewarded. You are too shrewd to be drawn into arguments about pointless theories for which there are no data, only conjecture. In addition you have correctly surmised that I like to talk. I freely admit it. Especially when one can find such a receptive and discriminating ear. Which of us doesn't want to believe we have something significant to say? I am no different unless perhaps I am even more convinced of it than most. If it were not so I would have given up long ago and been forced to accept that my life has counted for nothing. Call it arrogance, pride, egotism—or just absurdity. It doesn't much matter; whenever I find someone willing to listen, I talk.

This bar is full of them. They have endowed these chairs which we occupy at their generosity. Each of them at one time or another has sat where you are now and indulged me. One by one they have found my disclosures less and less entertaining, more and more a recital of life as it is, as they see it around them or have tasted it for themselves, until finally, bored, they drift away to their own pursuits, those same pursuits that I have so painstakingly described for them. Usually they leave over some small disagreement, brought on by the fact that they do not want to face the truth; or they are embarrassed by it, or it is too painful, or they find it comical, or disgusting. Yet it is not me they run away from, but life. I merely hold it up for them to see again for themselves, some for the first time. Regrettably, it is only too easy to go through life with one's eyes closed, to live but never be truly alive.

They leave, yes, but not before they come to realize that I am right. Faced with the present danger they cannot bring themselves to also face the truth of that awful realization. Tragically they miss the point and give up too soon, just when it is becoming possible to put the whole thing into perspective, to collect the reward of their labors and at last to view life as it might be. I suppose it is comic in a sense. But it is also tragic, the one true human tragedy. By what they do next they prove nevertheless that I am right in my assessment; that they have without knowing it understood my message all the same, and leave to act it out for themselves; to behave as if they understood perfectly the image I was holding up to them, the point of life as it should be.

And what is that? The question is written all over your face, my friend. It is really quite simple, practically inescapable. No, it is not learned. I don't teach it, nor can anyone except by example. We are born with it, or all of it that we can ever know anything about. But I am getting ahead of myself. We will come to the point, in due course, as you so aptly put it. What? Will I be able to convince you? You already believe it, I assure you. And is it indeed the truth? In the end I don't know about the truth, my friend. Like all the others I rely mainly on hope.

Come though, it has grown very late and even philosophers must have some respite. If you wish to continue you will find me here again in this same place tomorrow, and every night. It is a simple message I bear, and straightforward, but a lengthy one. Your chair will be reserved and waiting for you. Once you accept the appointment it is yours until you choose to relinquish it.

May I treat you then to one last drink of the evening, to commemorate this beginning? Do not trouble yourself; he is bringing them now. I took the liberty of signaling him earlier, on the presumption that you would have the same as before. Custom can be such a comfort in these times. Without it, virtually nothing is certain. I have come to greatly admire it, and to rely on it.

Would I please point out for you which one is the owner? Why, I thought you might have guessed, my friend: I am the owner. Yes, this is my *Act IV.* There is no finer stage, or truer, to be found anywhere.

2

Ah, you have returned for another evening, my friend. I am most gratified. I had every confidence you would. But still, you do me a great honor. I have been looking forward to it since we parted last evening. I trust that you rested well and made the most of your day. Never mind. Here in the desert, the evenings are their own reward.

Tell me, have you seen our city at night? Step out on the terrace with me and away from this smoke-filled din.

There, that is much better. It is so clear here at night in the desert; cool and refreshing, even on the hottest of days like this one. Ours is a thin and rarefied air—breathe it in deeply. Doesn't it make you feel vigorous and exhilarated just to fill your lungs with it? It has its own vitality, not at all like the oppressive vapors of the lowlands—more like the pure air of mountains, but without the harshness.

I first came to this place several years ago, during Nativity. In winter, temperature inversions cause the air to hang stagnant over this valley, and when I stepped off the airplane the incense of pinon and juniper from a thousand fireplaces greeted my nostrils. Where I had expected the sharp metallic odor of kerosene and jet fuel I found instead the hazes of ancient fires still lingering in the night air, the way they had long before the Europeans ever came to this land: those of the Anasazi and the pueblo dwellers who greeted the conquistadores; also those of the streams of settlers who came afterwards, the prospectors and miners, the ranchers and farmers, merchants and businessmen, the builders of towns and cities right up to the present moment. When I reached my hotel I did not go to bed but roamed the streets until early in the morning, like an incense-drugged wanderer—the entire city smelled like one of those scented Christmas candles—peering curiously into shop windows, looking wide-eyed at the decorations, delighting in the festive mood of crowds. Nowhere had I seen so many beautiful young lovers, nor felt such yearning myself.

The next day dawned bright and clear—the desert air was cold and brisk, the sun golden and warm. The endless sky was a breathtaking blue, deep and jewel-like and I could see forever in any direction I looked. Ever since that first encounter this has been a magical place for me. No matter where else I have gone I always come back eventually—here to the desert where it all began. Who knows? Perhaps I am back this time for good; perhaps, my friend, we all are.

If so, then no regrets. The desert is the proper place for harsh realities—its majestic serenity and timelessness can endure and transcend them. See those lights on the ridge of mountains behind us? Those peaks have lasted for hundreds of millions of years. They were formed in a cataclysmic underwater upheaval when this land was covered by an ancient sea that left the tops of those mountains encrusted with limestone and fossilized shells. They lay covered by water for millions of years and even now have not completely dried out, still weeping springs that cascade down the sides of them to vanish as a trickle in the desert below. Few of those boulders on the slopes have changed their positions during the relatively brief time we have existed—none since we first crept out of our caves and began farming and building cities and constructing civilizations—and they will occupy those same positions long after we have vanished.

It is sobering to think of it, my friend. To have rising up out of the desert at the very edge of this magnificent city such a towering monument to the puny insignificance of *Homo sapiens*, leering down at us from all those brooding, silent, skull-like stones. Yet it is inescapable. One can choose to ignore it, or not, but nothing can alter the fact of it. Nor do we need a science to convince us. On any day one can experience insignificance in the silent indifference of these rocks. It is a truth that does not deceive, spoken to us out of the eternal wisdom of the desert.

All around you are monuments sculptured out of those same truths. Those ancient volcanos to the west have known the scours of countless grains of sand, blown by the winds each spring for countless centuries; and the splash of equally many raindrops from summer thunderstorms, which have combined with the wind to weather and shape them into that insignificant pile of rubble we see. These arroyos and the flat-topped mesas bordering them mark the course of ancient streams and the pathways of now-stilled breezes, that together, grain by grain, removed the soil and left their outlines in its place. Yet each year after the melting snow has run its course and the spring winds have subsided, they still look the same to us, and they will continue to do so when the last human trace has been eroded and weathered away.

Is it not a vast comfort to be reminded of it? Yes, there is a strange contradiction in it. Call it the illusion of certainty in a precarious existence, or the futile hope of glimpsing our own immortality carved in the eternal stones, but it is a solace nonetheless. That we could exist at all in a world where there is the permanence and stolidity of stone is heartening, my friend.

Too, there is a distinctive quality of light in the desert, brimming and implacable in its many moods—soft and seductive at dawn; shimmering and expansive by midday; at dusk, subtle and translucent—that shows up the truth relentlessly in all its shades and nuances. Here certainty and truth converge and one can see clearly what elsewhere is only guessed at or hoped for. Surrounded by such stern splendor, such imposing calm, one can confront truths too severe to be reconciled otherwise, hold them up to view without hopelessness or despair. Yes, the desert holds special promise for those threatened. It is liberating and redeeming, and in its vast emptiness is the fulfillment of our most urgent yearnings. A single day amidst its expanses may yield more truth than an entire lifetime in less sensual surroundings.

But let us make no mistake, my friend. We are not concerned with escape but with reality. All of this natural splendor is but a backdrop to our real interest. See how brightly the stars shine in the desert, pure and undiminished. Yet for all their beauty they are no more wondrous than those thousands of man-made lights that dot the valley below us. From atop the nearby mountains they can be seen stretching for miles in every direction; in the clear night air they rival the stars themselves for our admiration. I came from up there on the mountain earlier this evening. On those days when my business allows it I catch a late tram, remaining on top until after dark to watch as, one by one, the lights emerge from the desert floor, little islands of lingering daylight in the surrounding darkness, transforming the surface of the earth, like a mirror, to nocturnal images of the heavens. Surely in these dangerous times, my friend, it is not for ourselves individually that we fear. Each of us realizes our own fate. It is for all those lights collectively, and what they represent, that we are concerned.

See how passionately they twinkle and blaze in the darkness. Even in the more unfortunate sections of the city—I hesitate even to mention it in the face of such dazzling beauty—in the slums, there is nowhere any break in the lights. They shine their promise the same on good and bad alike. Each tiny shimmering point represents some flickering spark in our brains that gave rise to the spectacle before us, that created these cities and the civilizations they weave out of so many individual dreams and striving.

It is not an absurdity, as some would have us believe, but our own special reality. What you see in front of us is what it is all about. The world for us is no longer a wilderness of primeval and pristine places, but a civilization of cities. We created them; and having done so we cannot very well deny them. This is what we have wanted for ourselves, what we have worked so long and hard to achieve. The streets are littered with refuse and the plaster in places is crumbling, but we do not really want to abandon them for some false nostalgia. Even Thoreau built with nails and hewn boards and periodically strode back into that society he denounced but had no intention of abandoning altogether. We know our condition only by holding it up to something else. The current of history for which we are a tributary flows between banks bordered by cultivated fields and factories, and littered with garbage and rusting automobiles and broken bottles. If what you see before you did not exist we would simply create it anew for ourselves, the way we have labored for centuries to do, all the while complaining bitterly and imagining utopias that would merely replace one reality with another, equally unfulfilling one. Those who see in our present danger the reflections of these lights as the cause are peering in the wrong mirror. The correct likeness is rather our own. They mistake symptom for cause.

That is the first realization I came to, my friend; all the others followed from it.

Shall we go back inside and order drinks? This night air is over-stimulating; too much beauty leads one to become idealistic. There, that too is much better. I have developed a fondness for their babble; and the smoke burns my eyes and reminds me that I am alive. For too long I tried to be what each of them would become. Now I am content to be simply what each of us is.

I came to that first realization naturally enough. You see, before I took up confessing nightly on this stage I was a member of the technical establishment. If you prefer labels: a *scientist-technician*; that compound designation, since the distinction has been blurred beyond recognition. That which is only technique passes routinely nowadays for science. *Homo faber* is mistaken for *Homo sciens*. No one differentiates, and all of technology is labeled science—a confusion of cause for effect. We are a society of technicians, not scientists. We are good at doing, but we disdain true understanding. Perhaps we are pragmatists and realize that the one is not essential to the other. We will leave understanding to those more able to deceive themselves. If so then we are wiser than the scientists and those who only think they have found understanding, and I misjudge.

More likely though it is a matter of mistaken awe. The bomb goes off and we find ourselves standing in the shadow of our idols; and they shine too ominously in that glare. We are fearful, and having been seized by our fear we have come to fear everything the same.

Who much cares whether it is science or technology that dooms us, or only those who in their ignorance and greed and blind disregard make bad use of them? One doom is as irreparable as another, and survival may as often belong to the wary as to the aggressor. There are many strategies for surviving; fear may be quite effective for a while. We recoil from any suggestion of cowardice as a virtue; and abhor any image of ourselves as less than heroic. But it is not clear anymore who the real heroes are, and caution is another matter entirely. We need time to sort things out. "Blessed are the wary for they shall inherit the earth." It may be a maxim to live by. Ah, yes, my able friend—most appropriate indeed: "Discretion is the better part of valor." Clearly we have been there before, and "there is nothing new under the sun."

Regardless, I know that you understand the difference; so I will tell you that in my case I have been at various times both scientist and technician, and many other things besides. And not immodestly, I submit that I have done them all with some distinction.

I came to it naturally, in a manner of speaking: by an accident of birth you might say. An inquiring nature was evident in my temperament from an early age. And I had the good fortune to be born to generous parents who indulged me in my pursuits, and to have grown up out of doors in the fresh air and sunshine, in a small rural community. As a child I was allowed to be alone, almost solitary, and I lived out my fantasies in private, uninhibited in the development of my imagination.

From the beginning I was the product of a number of competing influences. A part of me dreamed of a romantic past filled with adventure and unspoiled wilderness—I read *Robinson Crusoe* and *Treasure Island*, and the novels of Sir Walter Scott and James Fenimore Cooper. In my dreams I lived the life of the innocent savage and longed for a return to a more pristine time, unfettered by any concerns except those that were the object of my adventures.

My days were spent roaming the countryside. Every woodlot became a forest, every pond a lake, every insignificant stream a river to be followed toward some awaiting adventure. I learned to hunt. Not with firearms—that would have been a denial of my fantasy—but with slingshot and spear and with bow and arrow, whatever implements of antiquity I could fashion for myself out of materials readily available and could teach myself to use. I became a naturalist. Soon I could identify the common birds and plants and animals I encountered in my wanderings, and had turned to field guides to satisfy my longing to know more. I discovered there another aspect of myself: an innate and insatiable curiosity about the nature of things which was the natural instinct of the scientist.

Then somewhere along the way I read about the stars and began to dream of space travel and the unlimited possibilities of other worlds entirely. The romanticism of the past gave way to that of the future. From the natural man of Rousseau emerged the scientist of an equally romanticized tomorrow. Is it not the case? Science has assumed the mantle of the new romanticism. These scientist-technicians imagine themselves pragmatic realists, but aren't they merely indulging in romantic flights of fancy? The true realists are those for whom no amount of science or technology can alleviate their suffering and misery; indeed for whom it often brings on more. Every speculation serves merely to avoid the necessity of facing what cannot be immediately altered. The only realism is that of the moment, from which any escape is equally romantic.

Yet I was a dreamer, able to move freely between my dreams and that other reality until at last the two merged and I drew no distinction between them. I made my escape into the future just as effortlessly as I once had into the past—both relied on the same quality of imagination. From natural history to natural philosophy was but a short step. I explored the physical phenomena of the world around me, learned about the laws of motion and the principles of electricity and magnetism, about the science of thermodynamics and the oddities of the quantum theory. I digested speculations about the cosmos and the microcosm with equal relish.

It was then that I made a great discovery. Whereas the naturalists, it seemed, were mired down in cataloging an endless array of facts, the natural philosophers—the physicists—were onto a few simple principles that held out great promise and great seductiveness: that the universe might actually be understandable; that the same force that held the planets to their paths around the sun was responsible for the fall of an apple; that the laws determining the flow of current in a wire also explained the solidity of stone; and that all of it could be understood, and the universe made to surrender its profoundest mysteries to one individual in a single lifetime.

What would be required in exchange—all that would be required, I imagined—was to put aside every other concern. To dedicate oneself single-mindedly to the task without regard to the cost or consequences, whatever they might be, was where the bargain must be struck. It was a bargain as enticing to my young mind as it had been to all of the sorcerers and magi, the alchemists and Fausts before me. I was enthralled by the prospects of what such knowledge would bring; by the unlocked doors and inner secrets revealed; by the power it could bestow on whoever came to possess it.

Ah, but you smile. Truly; yet such are the imaginings and the idealism of youth, the optimism of every grand scheme untested. It is only later that another reality intrudes. Before one knows what one is up against anything is possible. Why else are the great discoveries in physics made before the passion of youth has subsided? Later on, one is bruised and becomes cynical, and no longer believes in the possibility. In retrospect it comes to seem more like the fortunes of luck, with each individual entitled to no more than a meager share.

What I discovered next however was more sobering. This success the natural philosophers enjoyed had been purchased at the price of a fatal compromise. In truth those shining principles which purported to explain everything, explained nothing. They were mere *descriptions* of what transpired, with never a hint of *why*, but only *how*, the planets moved and the apple fell. Oh, of course, by a deceptive slight of hand one thing was explained in terms of another, no less inexplicable, which then in a never-ending chain was itself explained in terms of something else, until at last the final quarry stood at bay in the shadows, just as dimly seen as what had originally been in need of illumination. Thus the apple fell and the planets moved because of gravity it was said; which in turn was explained as what made the apple fall and drew the planets together.

It was a clever and appealing deception, one that owed its success to a hard-bitten utility. In the precision of the calendar and the description of the night sky, in the exact knowledge of when to plant and when to harvest year in and year out, and the dates of the equinoxes, one could overlook that no one understood why the mysterious force could extend across the vast distances of space as easily as it reached up and plucked an apple from the tree. That it could not be explained more satisfactorily was unfortunate but even so it brought order to men's lives and bestowed on the world a reassuring predictability. And surely nothing of such overwhelming authority was ever a whim. In the accuracy of its predictions was the confirmation of a deeper truth going beyond mere description, a truth about the very nature of the universe and its causes, of which those things we observe are only the effects. Understanding is granted grudgingly; we will take it however it comes.

In my youthful optimism though, I determined not to give up so easily. There were more fundamental questions to grapple with. Clearly the universe must always have existed or else been created in some manner, but what had come before and what would follow were no less puzzling or intriguing for all that. I resolved to look more deeply at the causes of things.

Once more I returned to the past, this time with a difference. Now it was not a romantic nostalgia that drew me back but a thirst for the accumulated knowledge of the ages. I learned mathematics—read Euclid and studied analytic geometry and analysis. From there logic and deduction—the elements of pure reason—became my guide and ruling passion. I soon discovered that reason was the special province of the philosophers and I turned avidly to epistemology. I read voraciously but erratically.

In the tantalizing fragments of the Presocratics I encountered the first faltering efforts: those dark mysteries of Heraclitus; Empedocles's poem of eternal strife; the Oneness of Parmenides; Zeno's paradoxes. Afterwards the mature ripeness of Plato struck me as only a more eloquent and impassioned sophistry than that which Socrates decried. Aristotle was boring and in the Categories I did not find what I was looking for. Descartes delighted me but in the end was all too anxious to discard his doubts and rely on faith. I studied Hume and found his skepticism troubling; then Kant, whose reply upon being awakened from his dogmatic slumbers seemed only to assert what he was unable to demonstrate; then the early Wittgenstein, the Positivists, and others— the questions always the same, the answers ever elusive.

But never mind. I, like all of them before me, wanted to believe. If the truth was evasive it merely made the prize more coveted. I plunged in with renewed determination and commitment. Abstraction became for me the embodiment of perfection. In it I fancied that I had glimpsed the absolute—absolute truth and knowledge and wisdom—what the Greeks had termed virtue. What did it matter if it was only in my mind? At that moment all that mattered was what was in my mind. I had abandoned this reality for a more appealing one, my friend. The prospect of finally grasping the truth about something, about almost anything, of understanding it completely in a world of such palpable uncertainty and mystery, a world in which the single undeniable assurance is death and one's own mortality—that and the brief span of time allotted each of us to devote to the struggle—is the most alluring and corrupting influence I have known.

Look at them. See how earnestly they pursue their amusements. Each of them would agree—if not intellectually the way I experienced it at that moment, then certainly in their actions. It is only a matter of where we look for it. Some turn to simpler, more tangible pursuits; some search with their bodies and their senses rather than with their minds, but the quest is always there. We are driven to find some speck of certainty in all of this—no matter how pitiable—before we must die. The corruption of the intellect is that it—this speck of certainty—is found most easily there. There we can create a reality of our own choosing, where truth and belief can be interchanged freely to satisfy our longing for assurance, until we have mixed them up to where we can no longer distinguish between them—or want to.

It was a tidy world, satisfying and enticing, and I succumbed willingly to its artificial pleasures. I subscribed to any idealism; I became a philosophical realist. The mystical Forms of Plato, which earlier I had dismissed, those absolute abstractions of which everything in this world is but an imperfect copy, became not only real and attainable but the only reality or truth I acknowledged. I set aside every ugliness, denied any injustice. My senses feasted exclusively on the delights of my mind. Every puzzle became a challenge, every riddle answerable, reason held the key to every mystery.

Then one beautiful day in spring, as I strolled through the frenzied renewal of life all around me, I realized in a sudden seizure of inspiration the validity of the ontological proof of God: perfectibility undeniable. You no doubt know the argument, my friend. To deny existence to God, a perfect Being, is to deny one of the attributes of perfection. Before there can be any perfection there must first be existence. And I knew then and there with every fiber of my being that there *was* a God—that there *had* to be: reason demanded it and thus it was indisputable. If belief in God were only an act of faith, then reason itself was in jeopardy, and my world just a pretty bauble.

Alas, it was the beginning of the end—the threshold of my disillusionment. Opening the door to God brought with it compromises that undermined me. Such a God assumed responsibilities that seemed to me too unreasonable. There were the bitter realities that I had chosen to ignore: evil, suffering, death. Since I could find no denial of them in reason, I had to accept them—or compromise—and reason thereby took on a tarnished aspect. You know my dilemma well. Either there is an omnipotent God who is responsible for evil, or a more just God who is not all powerful and thus imperfect. I pursued the questions with sinking hopes. I became acutely aware of every injustice, the cry of every child, and the haunting, questioning eyes staring back at me. Where before I had never seen them I suddenly noticed derelicts shuffling aimlessly along the streets; an old woman begging on a street corner; mothers with ragged children peering desperately into store windows at Christmas time.

Then the final and most crushing blow of all: I fell in love; and the first person whom I had ever wanted to possess with all my soul and being was denied to me. Moreover I was forced to look on, helpless, as others possessed her, others to whom she gave herself freely, mocking me in my desolation. I was devastated. The world was dark and empty. Beside it, reason seemed only an inadequacy, incongruous, incapable of any solace.

I grew cynical. Perhaps these philosophers were only speaking nonsense. Perhaps what we witness is without reason or purpose, except in our hopes as a blind act of faith, powerless against the crush of a cruel world. If I had been so easily deceived once I could not trust myself a second time. I accepted that there were questions with no answers, for which reason alone was inadequate. And where reason had failed there could be no sure guide as to what would work. These philosophers were merely foolish, I concluded. It is not possible to understand the causes of things. All that can be known is what we observe and can demonstrate for ourselves. The scientist is right after all. The world must first be described and those principles by which it operates identified and spelled out. Out of that description, and from it alone, would emerge whatever understanding is possible. And so I turned my back on metaphysics as folly and dedicated myself solely to science.

What are you thinking, my friend? Does it sound in retrospect like little more than the miscarriages of youth? Perhaps so, but the innocence of youth imparts its own wisdom. Few lessons are ever truer or more enduring than those acquired early. Nothing subsequently has changed my judgment of it, except that now I might further condemn reason in my indictment.

Why should that surprise you? Can we not more easily accept the utter futility of everything in this world than cling to the illusion that reason holds any meaning for us? Judged by reason it is a foolish world, and a capricious one, in which we are titillated and tantalized with a few brief moments of bittersweet pleasure that we may have our hopes dashed in the end. It is not the world that has somehow gone wrong but rather our insistence on reason. It is we that have fallen from grace through our elaborate deceptions to keep from facing the truth.

How might I answer your charge that I lost heart and gave up too soon? Death is not too soon, my friend. Every philosopher has met death empty-handed. None has ever found that truth they professed to believe possible. They have spoken volumes, though obscurely, about the *possibility*—but always just the possibility—never getting beyond that fatal self-deception. After this many failed attempts it is simply pointless. What no one can succeed in doing does not remain a possibility, except in a philosopher's dream. Wittgenstein spoke the best advice: "About which one can say nothing, one should remain silent." There the matter rests.

Look at them: they have no need of it anyway, this mealymouthed speculation of philosophers. Nothing any philosopher has ever had to say is of the least concern at this moment. We must *live* our lives, not *argue* about them endlessly. Why should we believe any of these philosophers when the best they can manage is to ask the same questions that each of us must face every minute of each day? They hide behind words and fancy phrases that say nothing; but we must choose, and having chosen we cannot escape the consequences. There is no truth, my friend, other than that each of us comes to know as the *living truth*—which needs no proof beyond that knowledge of it we live day by day. Still it is enough; it sustains us.

No, I assure you, I did not become bitter, believe me; nor resigned either. There is a disillusionment without bitterness. It is the quality of acceptance necessary to embrace the truth. Call it reality if you like. And certainly it is not inconsistent with hope. Without it one cannot truly have hope, which by comparison seems like only a more clever lie. I did not feel bitterness, but the relief one experiences at dispensing with a foolish preoccupation. In the thwarted attempt to find the truth I had at least found some truth.

Moreover, there were other considerations in my life. There were the painful realities of growing up. One had to get along. Ever present was the nagging question of what I would become. There were compromises to be made: in an inequitable society those more fortunate must learn to look the other way. It is necessary to play the game according to the rules, to conform, to fit in. As I said, one must learn to get along.

One does not think too seriously about it when growing up. And I was more fortunate than many. I was born into a social class that bestowed privileges and could manipulate affairs to its own advantage. My parents had forged the basis of a good life and could simply pass it along to me. All that was required was that I likewise embrace those values on which it was founded—that I not bite the hand that fed me—and this I did easily enough. Acceptance is a passive act, and it was convenient not to question too closely what was happening around me.

I enjoyed my quiet days of solitude in the sunshine, left to my own thoughts, and I welcomed them guilelessly. There were many happy moments made possible by those I loved and respected. Why should I have questioned their motives or intentions? I was their beneficiary, and even if I did not reflect on that realization often, or at any length, it could not have escaped my notice entirely. I looked about me and everywhere there was acceptance of one's condition, even by the unfortunate and oppressed. Such acquiescence was justification of the status quo. No one seemed personally responsible. What I observed was the natural order of things, and everyone appeared resigned to make the best of it. Only later would I come to know that awful silence in which human longing is rooted. For the moment I heard mainly the laughter, loudest of all my own.

By the time I had developed doubts (guilt is a form of doubt, is it not?) I had succeeded in implicating an entire social order, and I consoled myself with their company. Churches, schools, teachers, the judiciary, the press—each an acknowledged symbol of authority and social responsibility—all conspired in the working of this society and none spoke too loudly or too pointedly about its evils. To do so would have endangered whatever advantage they—like myself—had gained by quietly looking the other way; the investment we all had in its continuation. It was either no evil at all, or the greatest evil imaginable; and to admit the latter would have been an act of desperation. This was a world devoid of heroes on either side.

I had embraced the reality of questions for which there are no answers, and these seemed like only more of the same. I resolved to avoid them as a meaningless frustration, to limit myself to what I could control and could know with some assurance. It seemed pointless to discuss what could never be decided. It is not that I was blind to injustice and suffering—once felt they are not easily forgotten—but I chose not to concern myself with them. Others could, and I believe that privately I was reassured when they did, though likely I would have argued that to do so was futile. I simply shut them out, and along with them everything that reminded me of them.

I avoided literature since it concerned itself with the human condition; and for the same reason, history and all political and social writings; and art and music as well. I confess that I could not understand art or what the artist was trying to express. And since I could not, I believed that in truth nothing of any importance was being said; that he was not talking about anything which had any real meaning or for which there was any hope of understanding or finding the truth. It was a pointless futility and too often a painful one.

The artist and his work were dismissed the same way metaphysics was before, as a kind of false knowledge beside which science held the only possibility of some more satisfying depiction of reality. The natural world did not talk back; nor did it ever disappoint since one approached it with no expectations. Whatever truths it yielded were always the same, and impersonal, and in that certainty I found the reassurance I felt missing from everything else. As I told you: I determined to become a scientist.

There was more than a chance element of security in that ambition. At one time a career in civil service or the law was the pathway to success. Now it was the scientist whose influence outstripped the others; the one on whom the others rely for whatever influence they still exert. The authority of the scientist is supreme. After all, my friend, the bomb does go off. The thing works—it is undeniable. And it casts its light alike on all these other miracles until everyone has become a believer, even if begrudgingly at times.

It was a lesson not lost on me. I had become adaptable. Not only that, I discovered in the process a latent talent for it, the ability to get along in the extreme. One might have been inclined to question whether I possessed any principles at all truly my own, so accommodating had I become to whatever circumstance or point of view I confronted. And I managed it with a show of sincerity that was beguiling. Mine was no unctuous obsequity, but a reassuring rapport. I may have been a chameleon, but my colors were convincing.

It was an act made easier by my willingness to place every other concern subordinate to the success of my methods. Matters of principle, of right and wrong, of morality, of the correctness or even the appropriateness of my behavior were subservient to the criteria of success. In my mind these other concerns only obscured the real issue by hiding behind unanswerable dilemmas and pointless paradoxes—those which I had previously set aside. In the matter of artful manipulation success was what mattered; and I had learned to be successful. With this new attitude I no longer viewed science as merely a valid source of knowledge, but as a powerful instrument for my own success—a fortuitous combination of the truth I had come to believe in and the success I recognized as necessary.

Earlier—I think it was about the time I first became disenchanted with philosophy—I had a vision of myself as merely an observer of this panorama, removed and peering down on it from somewhere else. It was, I believe, basically a scientific impulse. If I could not hope to understand the human element of this existence then I would satisfy myself with observing and cataloging it, as something of a natural historian of the human condition; separate and thus risking nothing, yet able to search for whatever meaning I could find in describing the drama. I recall the enormous feeling of relief at the thought of being removed from it, yet not totally; of being able to witness the unfolding of events without having to take the risks and pay the too often painful price demanded by my participation.

When I confided this impulse to a young woman with whom I had a brief infatuation she chided me and lectured me on my responsibilities, doubting at first my sincerity and then questioning my motives. When I tried to convince her she would not hear of it, putting it down as cowardly and beneath me, a betrayal of my moral obligations. That I would even conceive such a concept, she said, revealed an imagination too fertile to waste in carrying it out. Instead, she argued, one must strive to make some positive contribution using whatever talent one has been given.

I hadn't anticipated the fervor of her reaction and to tell the truth I was more than a little amused by the storm of protest she raised. After all, I didn't ask to be here in the first place, and anyone was free to quit at any time. What I was proposing was a compromise of sorts, an intermediate position, not for everyone but of no great harm for a distinct few.

Yet in the end her protests were telling. Perhaps it was a measure of the extent to which I had become conditioned by growing up in this society, some sense of values that I had unwittingly subscribed to in the process and which her imprecations touched. Whatever it was, her objections shattered my confidence. I hadn't asked to be here but that made little difference. I was here, and I could either stay or not, but I couldn't have it both ways. And by being here one incurred a debt not lightly dismissed. You see, my friend, I hadn't given up hope after all. No, far from it; I stood at the threshold of preparing myself for what I was about to become. Whatever spark of humanity I may have wanted to ignore was there nevertheless, waiting to find an outlet, if not in lofty thoughts then in good works.

I do not know any more than you where these urges of decency originate—whether we are born with them or only learn them later. I suppose it is a pointless question. However we acquire them, there they are. Has there ever lived anyone so hardened that the laughter of a child or the smile of another person has not at some time made a difference? I for one cannot imagine it.

And in our pursuit of decency we have the origin of much that we find troubling, much of what we falsely attribute to evil. What produces some harm is not necessarily evil. Decency is too generous an urge for such pedantic quibbling. Decency is broad enough to encompass all human hopes and striving—along with courage, honor and truth, love and compassion, also ambition, pride and desire; even at times greed, mistrust and deception, or worse. It is of no use to say these things cannot be decent when they cause harm or lead to the wrong result— that assumes we can know the consequences of our actions beforehand or that we can understand the basis of our behavior. If it were possible perhaps we wouldn't be in this situation. No one consciously set out to doom us; and if we have done so it was for other purposes altogether, most of which seemed well-intentioned at the outset. Getting ourselves into this predicament was not that simple. It would be foolish to expect salvation in simple solutions.

I will say it again, my friend: what we see around us is what we have wanted for ourselves. It is not some cruel joke or gargantuan mistake, but purposeful. Purchased at great sacrifice and dedication and longing, bit by tiny bit, one day at a time against all imaginable odds and every conceivable obstacle; in the face of death and denial and deprivation, at the cost of pain and suffering incalculable; but also in great joy and hope and celebration. To deny it is to deny ourselves outright. We may not like the face in the mirror that fate has dealt us, but it is indisputably our own.

To be here in the evenings for drinks and conversation—it is what I have chosen. I must believe there is some value in it, even if it is only because I am able to choose it and I can indulge myself. Does that make it indecent? If our existence is to be that precarious then it will be snatched from us anyway and passed along to some creature more adamantine than our soft species, and thus it is nothing worth groveling after in fear and shame. Better to live in hope and let the truth take care of itself.

Ah, notice there—the full moon just rising above the mountains. That means for some time now, while we were still in its shadow, it has been visible in the valley beyond. Come, let us move out to the terrace where we may sit and enjoy the view for ourselves.

Tell me, has there ever been a spectacle to equal this one? Look at that sky, even at night shimmering and palpable with a glow like that of a black jewel—one feels drawn into its vastness; and the outlines of the mountains looming above us, softened by the darkness; the cold night air on one's face; the sighing of wind through the pines. No depiction is ever adequate. If it has not been experienced it cannot be truly imagined; once encountered, it is afterwards unforgettable in some inner chamber of our being.

We are still part of this too, and nothing you see around you or in the valley below is any denial of it either. The tinkle and clatter of glasses from within carries well on the night air and mixes easily with the stars and the sounds of crickets and whip-poor-wills, just as we hear the echo of some more human flute-like music in the singing of the hermit thrush at dusk. There is no clear demarcation between us and the rest of everything. The fallacy of this other world we have created for ourselves and which we wear like a protective mantle is that we become too easily blinded to that realization.

Excuse me, my friend, but look up there. Just above the ridge in the moonlight you will see hang-gliders maneuvering in the winds that ride up these slopes. Do you see them? Yes, there are several. They launch from the crest, by stepping off the sheer rock faces and into the bottomless canyons wedged into the side of the mountain, mostly by day, but apparently these are in search of some greater adventure. Any feat once accomplished becomes a challenge to be surpassed. They will stay aloft as long as possible by riding back and forth on the wave of cold air spilling over the top, before eventually gliding down to a landing at the foot of the mountain.

But of course it is dangerous—do you recall the story of Icarus? Frankly, for some that is its appeal. Yet even from here they are beautiful, circling in the moonlight. More than beautiful—inspiring. Who could witness it without feeling a sense of wonder at the achievement, at the sight of this fragile earthbound creature soaring at that height in the night sky like a winged god out of mythology? It is one of man's earliest longings—to fly free and unfettered as the birds. Yet it was not done like Daedalus and Icarus, with feathered wings, but with wire and metal tubing and nylon cloth in a contraption that looks like it might have sailed right out of the pages of Leonardo da Vinci's sketchbooks. If he could see it, Leonardo would understand perfectly and would weep tears of joy at its realization.

The longing that you see circling above you in the night sky has been building ever since the original spark in man's mind triggered this outpouring, and produced the works dotting the plains below us or which lie decaying in the soil below that, and that one day will cover up even what we have made for ourselves. In the presence of such yearning—at the sight of a hang-glider in the moonlight—we are uplifted and moved to see in our possibilities a hope that transcends our puny insignificance, that gives us some momentary belief in ourselves.

But at what price is it purchased? How many open-pit scars in the earth were required for the ore that made the wire and metal tubing? How many Arab women and children were put at risk for the oil that went into the nylon covering? What pollution now flows toward the sea or reddens the sunset as a result of the manufacture of it all? And what sorrow will result when it fails and dashes that same hope and yearning lifeless against the ground? At what point should we begin to count the cost too dear—to feel the shame of our passions? When does all of this overstep the decency of human striving and become hubris and folly, the final act in one more irrevocable human tragedy?

The answers, my friend? No one can give you the answers. They must come from life itself.

3

I am glad you have come early this evening, my friend. We will have a chance to sit on the terrace and watch the sunset. Come, he will bring us our drinks outside.

Yes, it was truly hot today—even those who are defensive about the virtues of our climate would be forced to admit it. In consideration of the heat I ordered us something cool, with crushed ice. We can revert to our usual libations later if you prefer. You like these local concoctions made of tequila, do you? Well, let us drink then: to tradition.

In this arid climate I find I do not mind the heat—it suffuses the muscles with a vernal warmth and imparts an invigorating suppleness. It is the closest I have felt to being permeated with that vital force we draw from the sun. Besides, the sun will soon slip below the horizon and we will be plunged once more into the soothing cool of evening. At this elevation the earth cools off quickly, and heat and light go hand in hand.

During the warm months this is perhaps my favorite time of day—just to sit here tranquil in the fading warmth and watch the sunset, reflecting on the events of the day, or anticipating those of the morrow. Memory and imagination: together they define us, do they not? No knowledge without the one, no thought without the other. Aristotle regarded man as a rational animal, for the curious reason that he could do sums; but he was wrong. How these philosophers have wanted to believe at every turn that our uniqueness lay in the ability to solve a few pointless puzzles. The discomfort in such a view is that it suggests a place for us only if the world is truly rational, yet who can ever be sure of it?

Does what you see before you appear rational? Men have sat and looked upon it for centuries without being able to agree. Most have wanted to believe. Others have been unconvinced—some openly suspicious of that desire we have to solace ourselves with delusion.

For my part, I confess that I see in its ordered patterns of streets and buildings, in the flow of traffic and the collective activities of its inhabitants, no more and no different rationality than that of an anthill. The one is about as easily disrupted as the other. As for survival, the record speaks for itself and favors the ants. And it would seem to demand an unusual detachment to regard the obliteration of this global consciousness contemplating itself as an act of any great rationality.

Whether or not the world is rational is of no consequence. Man himself is not a rational animal. Man is a reflective creature—with the capacity to regard his situation. Perhaps it amounts to more than that, but his other accomplishments are still too puny or short lived for us to draw any conclusion. In a universe as limitless as this how else are we to gauge significance except by comparison? Less than a century after grasping the concept of our own evolution as a species, some were ready to claim that we had taken our fate out of the hands of circumstance and were in control of our destiny—that we could rise above natural law. I suppose they are not impressed by the knocking at our door. Perhaps they didn't understand Darwin.

But notice what a truly spectacular sunset, my friend—one of those rare wonders of natural beauty for which the desert is so renowned. See how it reddens to a deep ruby tint, as if the sky were dripping blood. Have you ever seen one more beautiful?

Yes, I agree, it does look almost unnatural, doesn't it? It is just a little too spectacular. That is the reason I pointed it out. These sunsets we are having lately are enhanced by the eruption of a small volcano in the tropics, a rather insignificant pimple on the side of the earth, virtually ignored at the time. A minor geologic event, no different from hundreds of others occurring each century; except that this one spewed copious quantities of sulphur into the atmosphere and reddened sunsets throughout the middle latitudes in the northern hemisphere. It is thought the effect could persist for months, even years.

Yes, it is beautiful—regardless of how it was caused. But let me ask: Is it a natural sunset? I think we would have to agree it is as natural as any other that occurs. Are those that we produce by our own pollution then any less natural? They are certainly going to be no less spectacular once we have poured enough oxides of sulphur into the air. And if the carbon dioxide level increases to the point where the earth warms and the polar ice caps melt, will the resulting floodplains along the Atlantic seaboard, or the tropical vegetation growing here be any less natural? How could they be? We are part of nature; we and everything we do are as natural as horseflies—someone has said it. Or that forest fire burning on the side of the mountain; does it matter whether it was started by lightning, or by a careless hiker? Would either have been avoidable or distinguishable in the end? What difference is there in being bitten by a disease- carrying insect, or by the addict's needle? Both exact their toll.

It could all be caused as easily—the red sunsets, the disruption of life—at any moment by the impact of a large meteor. It has happened before, and it will again someday. There are estimates of the frequency of occurrence, evidence of past collisions, some suggestion that the dinosaurs may have been adversely affected. What assurance do we have that we would survive it? Why then does it matter if we only suffer our fate from some other cause or have a direct hand in it ourselves? Either way it is part of nature, no less than we are part of nature. And either way it is still the truth: that which comes to be. The truth, in retrospect, has a way of being unavoidable.

Would I argue then that everything is permissible? No, certainly not; that too would be a refutation of the truth—it seems that only one outcome is allowed. In determining what is attempted, however, the issue is not as plain, and everyone may try to influence the result in their own way. I am not advocating a philosophy of passivity or resignation— merely cautioning against one of despair.

It is the attitude of those I described earlier by the label scientist- technician, though they would vehemently deny it. To them the difference is that any desired outcome is possible. Difficulty in itself is no obstacle, nor are considerations of subtleties. No matter that there is no way of even knowing which goals have merit. The more desirable some result is deemed, the more attainable it becomes. Those outcomes that can be made to appear possible only by the most unlikely and difficult of circumstances become the most desirable of all. The possibility of some unforeseen consequence is put out of mind entirely—or dismissed as an acceptable risk in the overall scheme of things.

There is a need on the part of those with this mentality to feel in control at all times. They are compensated in this longing by the steadfast conviction that no problem is beyond the solution of better technology— and further compensated by believing that trying to solve those that may be beyond solution is still preferable to doing nothing in the face of some perceived threat.

These are the modern managers of their own technological destiny—and along with theirs, ours too. They view the future as a mechanistic juggernaut, advancing unimpeded in obedience to the inexorable will of history. And they are not to be held responsible if one or two are accidentally crushed along the way—least of all if some "natural" process which they do not regard themselves part of is disrupted.

In their view managing a technological existence can be no different from managing any other enterprise. The principles are identical—only the objects being manipulated change. Isn't every problem at heart the same: some question amenable to analysis, by which a logical solution is affected, before moving on to the next question? What works so well in exploiting the atom must undoubtedly work when applied to the economy, or the environment. Surely the power that produced the devastating roar of the bomb cannot be intimidated by the lowly clank and hum of machinery, or the bumbling of a bureaucracy.

And in elevating it to a science of management they have made of it an ethic—practically a moral imperative. It has become untenable to sit idly by, while what can be shaped by technology is allowed to proceed undirected. We have all known them. Give them any job, no matter how subordinate, and immediately they insist on change. It is immaterial what was done before—it isn't ever good enough. Otherwise they could not be made to feel indispensable. Better still if they can depict their predecessors as bungling and incompetent in order to embellish their own actions. Every change once implemented is held up as pivotal, as having solved some problem that, though non-existent, was too obstinate for anyone but themselves.

They become obsessed with leaving their mark, with placing their stamp on things, like some mindless dog lifting its leg at the bidding of instinct around the boundary of its territory. Failure to do so is a sign of managerial weakness. They exult in the chance to make decisions, few of which need ever have been made at all. Whatever purpose or function the job had in the first place becomes secondary to their conduct of it. The worst succumb to their own egomania. They expect effusive praise for every little thing that goes right. The mess they make of everything else is excused by the difficult nature of the circumstances, or by how bad things were when they took over, or if all else fails, by talking about how much worse things would have been except for them.

Forgive me, my friend, but you have touched a raw nerve. I do not mean to be uncharitable; nor do I overestimate the impact of such pompous conceit in the larger scheme of things. I have never subscribed to the belief that events are shaped solely by men. The object of my scorn is the contemptible arrogance of this attitude, the swagger and self-assurance of those it afflicts—the deplorable lack of insight and intellect that it signals. I confess, as you may have guessed, that I have suffered at the hands of such fatuous boobs. Sometimes, when I consider the wasted years, I become bitter and indulge in a momentary lapse—it will quickly pass.

In reality there is little cause for resentment. The behavior I describe is only a refinement of a more basic instinct. With a gun to our heads which of us would sit idly by and do nothing? From the first time prehistoric man picked up a stone to hurl as a projectile, or sharpened a stick in the fire to use as a spear, he was displaying the instinct to manage things. By the time he had banded together with others of his kind and planted crops and built settlements, he had become, henceforth and forevermore: *Homo ministerium.* Can we blame him for doing what has always been to his advantage? Likely we would not be here enjoying our drinks otherwise, and at this moment I would count that a loss. It is foolish to expect that any trait so advantageous to our survival would not become refined to the degree we see it, or persist so tenaciously as a characteristic of the species. Every virtue is tiresome in excess.

Still, these managers are insufferable somehow! I suppose it is because I have grown suspicious of hypocrisy and the idea of manifest destiny. The most self-righteous among them actually come to believe in the correctness of what they are doing. They regard their actions as virtuous, instead of admitting that they only do it for the same reason that we fornicate or masturbate. Because it feels good and we enjoy it, and because there is an instinct in our loins that gives us the urge. They see their obsessive compulsion as the special destiny for which millions of years of evolution have prepared us, and which we have an inescapable obligation to fulfill. Our situation, in their view, does not serve as a refutation of their ethic, but as its further confirmation. If we had managed our affairs better we would not be in the present predicament—and the only hope for us lies in wiser management in the future. I am as tired of their moral preachments as I am unimpressed by the strength of their accomplishments. The best they can manage is to point out how much worse things might have been. There! I have gotten it out of my system. I will say no more about it.

I hope I have not offended you, my friend. For all I am aware you may consider yourself among those I berate. Are they not in control everywhere? If I may appeal to your charity, remember: we have been speaking here of the truth, which means the truth as each of us understands it. No offense is intended. The passion is my own, and genuine, but I assure you it is without malice. In spite of my outbursts, I pride myself on maintaining an open mind, though no longer to the point of innocence. Age has brought with it a certain cynicism which in youth would only have interfered with whatever else I managed to accomplish. Now it makes me more tolerant of views for which I once had little sympathy. But I am increasingly leery of those who claim to have the answers.

Observe how silently the night has stolen up on us. At this latitude twilight is brief, and darkness follows close on the heels of dusk. The natural beauty of the sunset has given way to the equally natural splendor of the city lights. The product of science? I would not dispute it. Certainly the impulse that gave rise to our longing to *know* more has led to our success in being able to *do* more, so why quibble over the matter of intentions? The lights are as dazzling either way. I drew the distinction earlier not to demean the curiosity that impels us to question why—nor to implicate it as the cause of our peril. Science is a noble passion, though one doomed at the outset to failure at the hands of its lofty aspirations.

Nevertheless I became a scientist. I would no longer be comfortable using that term to describe myself, but once it was true. I was led to it by all of the circumstances I have related to you. Still, it was not a fate thrust upon me by events or by my situation. It was a calling for which I was suited, and one I felt drawn to very early; almost from the first moment I had any inkling of science and the scientist—well before I had any mature comprehension.

My heroes have always been rebels. I confess they still are; more so now than ever. At that age I felt myself in rebellion against everything. I admired those independent spirits and free thinkers I encountered in my reading. When they can no longer threaten us we idolize them and hold them up to our youth as examples to be emulated, from the shelter of our own conformity. I keenly felt the truth of what they were saying and considered their words to be aimed directly at me. Later, when I had too much at stake to rebel openly, I continued to nurture a secret fondness for rebels and the spirit of rebellion.

Even now, whenever I am asked to give my address or telephone number, I delight in making them up at random, never giving out the same one twice and never using my own. I can do it with the most steadfast aplomb that no polygraph would detect any deception. I walk away from these encounters muttering 'fools!' under my breath, luxuriating in my momentary break with conformity and taking delight in the assertion of my will against those influences that would dominate and manipulate me.

I suppose you are right, my friend; some might think it childish, or foolish. But who gives a damn if the system works when whether it does or not, instead of the consequences, has become the foremost consideration? I change my telephone number often, and let it ring for no other reason than the inward satisfaction of not responding to its incessant mechanical beckon. Superfluous stop signs and traffic lights are another irritation. Whenever I can do so, I intentionally disobey them. Nothing gives me greater satisfaction. Revealing the full extent of my rebellious eccentricities might prejudice you against me. Just let me say that I regard myself a menace to that unchecked instinct for organized conformity that at times seems to have become the sole purpose of our existence.

Am I only being perverse, or petty, a laughable example of some self-destructive maladjustment? Ah, but it makes me feel good! If I must conform I will do so at least having known the satisfaction of defiance; even if I must suffer for it—no cause more noble! That first defiant cry of the newborn infant continues unabated in all of us throughout our lives; if not openly, then smoldering in some inner recess, to be extinguished only by death itself.

What will we do, my friend, when there are at last too many of us, or the means at our disposal too threatening, to tolerate any defiance of the collective will? When we can no longer safely indulge ourselves in wars, or dominance, or sex, or any of our traditional outlets? Will some new spirit of accommodation arise to save us? Will *reason* prevail? It will desert us as surely as it has those philosophers who put their faith in it. *Defiance* will solve the problem for us. Death will become our defiance.

Look around you. Is not the peril we feel in our present situation rooted in that instinctive realization? Which of us does not privately feel that we are already perched on the edge of that precipice, peering over into the grinning jaws of that leering countenance? Yet which of us is willing to surrender meekly? No—we will leap into the abyss flaunting our defiance. The cornered animal is always the most desperate, and we can only die once. If at all—then defiantly!

In the end it will not much matter whether nuclear holocaust, or some virus, or a sweltering planet dooms us; or whether we starve ourselves to death in a seething mass of humanity, or die choking in our own wastes; or succumb to some pestilence not yet evident. We can take comfort in the realization that we will not die of apathy, but lashing out and struggling to assert ourselves to the bitter end. This is not an attitude I owe to science, my friend, but one I acquired much later.

I can remember, from my earliest encounters, thinking of the scientist as rebel. The best of them have been of course: intellectual rebels—going against the prevailing doctrine to extend and refine our understanding of the world, in what has appeared from the beginning to be a natural progression toward some remote but attainable truth. I am thinking of those few who have made a profound difference: Galileo, Newton, and in our own century Einstein, and the small group of Europeans who created the quantum theory. There have been others, and deserving ones, but we have made these our symbols. They were rebels and fomenters of intellectual revolution. They asserted the right to think for themselves and to shatter traditions in the interest of a more perfect truth. And in each case there was opposition and rivalry and the clash of wills. Science is no exception, my friend.

In between these departures there have been long periods of conformity to accepted dogma; by the legions of followers content to extend an idea modestly or to probe its limits; or by those simply less fortunate in discovering any new and fruitful path. Ironically it is at this stage that science becomes the ultimate rebellion: rebellion against the world itself—and I became its most ardent rebel.

I professed my allegiance and threw myself into my studies. Every new thing that I learned brought ineffable joy and reassurance. Soon I had a reasonable foundation in the abstruse principles of mathematical physics, and bit by bit the pieces of the puzzle fell into place. I created for myself a world more perfect and satisfying than this one. A world of ideal point masses and frictionless motion, of mysterious pulls and tugs transmitted as if by magic across empty spaces. A world of harmonic oscillators and utter simplicity, in which what was too tiny to be seen could be imagined and invented at will, and what was not could be idealized and abstracted to conform to theory. It was a world all neatly expressed in tidy symbols on a piece of paper. Whatever wisdom the equations spoke the world performed, in perfect obedience to the intellect.

Those symbols became the bearers of truth and wisdom. They were both art and artifice: the ultimate expression of reality and truth and beauty; and at the same time the deception of all that is real. I worshiped at their shrine. I had them drawn upon my wall, in charcoal, like ancient hieroglyphics or some modern abstract art, symbolizing the span of man's efforts to fathom the world around him. Like all art, it was not necessary to understand them. Merely being in their presence was enough. More than one person who had no knowledge of their meaning was touched by their essential mystery, and confessed upon seeing them to feelings of reverence and awe.

I took refuge in their mystery and hid behind their meaning. I pretended to find in them a significance that others could never fathom. I employed them to my advantage. I delighted not only in what I knew, but in what others might not. I had discovered the corrupting power of knowledge. I relished the sense of omnipotence derived from knowledge, and the influence it bestowed over those whose ignorance made them fearful. I was corruptible; and I participated willingly in my own corruption.

Oh, but I truly wanted to believe, my friend—in that my motives were pure—I was sincere and devout. With me belief became an act of faith, a sacred duty. I elevated it to the status of a religion and served as its high priest.

I enjoyed myself immensely. I did not stay up sleepless nights on end, pouring over texts and proving theorems or solving problems, out of any sense of duty or obligation. I did not deny myself food or the company of others because I felt that truth must be served. Of course not. I did it because I loved what I was doing, because it satisfied some inner need and craving that I felt, to which I responded with all the desire and mania that the pleasure of its gratification brought me.

I was enamored with knowledge, with the inner satisfaction of knowing something for myself, of holding it in my mind and making it my own; with the sense of security and well being it provided; and with the power and influence and pleasure it promised.

In a word, my friend—I had reached maturity. That idealism I once courted in youth had found its mature outlet in self-indulgence. In this, why should I have been any different? That I might have expected better of myself merely betrays a youthful naiveté. I had discovered what any good cynic knows: every noble cause is founded on the greater need for gratification.

The edifice that I constructed and in whose temple I worshiped was that of classical physics. By the time I had progressed to the end of the nineteenth century in my studies, I had uncovered a world so satisfying in its concept, so ordered and predictable in its workings, that I had no desire to step out of it and over the threshold into the more troubling twentieth century. Across that intellectual horizon I could already see the disturbing loss of certainty that awaited me. The universe in which I stood functioned with clockwork precision and simplicity. God had made it and set it in motion, and it ran in perfect obedience to those few simple laws by which the hand of the creator was made manifest. It and everything in it were tending toward that state of ultimate perfectibility of which we were the obvious embodiment and intended heirs. What a consoling and reassuring concept, my friend. What treachery to have it torn from us—to be thrust from the security of our beliefs into the turbulence of this new age.

Of course a few minor problems remained. But none that in my faith I could not overlook, or for which it was worth destroying the entire edifice. There was the small matter of a slight discrepancy in the orbit of Mercury. And that minor mystery about forces reaching instantaneously across the empty vastness of space. Then there was the question of God's throne, or rather where exactly He had chosen to place it; the precise location of the favored spot at rest where He sat, immobile, looking down upon this universe He had created and set in motion.

There were always the speculations of philosophers to contend with, but these were easy enough to dismiss as idle musings. More troubling were the vexing questions of things too tiny, or too vast, to be seen; and of things supposedly at rest, or traveling infinitely fast, over which our own century found it necessary to set aside forever the reassuring certainty of this simpler world.

Once again I was the incurable romantic. In my nostalgia I could put out of mind what could not be seen. What was too vast to be known was no longer the proper domain of science but was better left to those— such as philosophers, or poets—given to flights of fancy. I would console myself with the precision of predicting the sunrise or a solar eclipse. See, my friend, the moon is just now rising again over the mountains—by my watch a little less than one hour later than we witnessed it last evening—in predictable and perfect obedience to natural law.

Faced with the intellectual upheaval that lay ahead of me, I clung romantically to the surety of the past. I wrapped it around me and listened in silence to the comforting beat of this mechanical clock, wound up at the moment of creation by a beneficent and wise creator to run smoothly and reassuringly forevermore. I would have been perfectly content to suspend time at the zenith of that golden age. I had ceased to be a scientist just as all those before me had likewise done at some point—at that instant when they first embraced a truth so shining and appealing that it transcended truth itself and became instead an article of faith, a belief to cling to at all cost, the last refuge in a changing world.

No, my friend, I am not discounting the triumphs of modern science—we have spoken of the bomb and eventually I was to encounter it myself. But at that threshold I think I sensed the loss of something more significant than just the immediate certainty of the past. It was the final loss of my innocence I faced, and a turning point in my life. I continued with my studies—becoming the physicist I had set out to be; even distinguishing myself after a fashion—but never again would I believe in the possibility of any certainty.

In the new science of the microcosm, the solidity of stone gave way to the void of Lucretius, filled with whirling swarms of atoms, neither particles nor waves but merely metaphor, a world invisible and unknowable. Those atomic particles, so hard and immutable to the Greeks, on closer scrutiny dissolved into resonant packets of energy, fuzzy and indistinct, interacting like waves on the surface of a pond. Their behavior could be described by those symbols on my wall, arranged in more clever and mysterious ways by any who knew the code, but to explain them one was reduced to poetry.

They behave now like waves and then again like particles, one was forced to admit. They possess size but no definite boundaries, and each is made of something else, which in turn is made of something else again, ad infinitum. But what are they really, the skeptic demands? One is forced to smile and say: "I do not know, my friend—it is a question one cannot ask", and to hold up first this image and then that one in the attempt to satisfy the curious longing.

All the while the cosmos drew in around me, no longer vast and infinite but confined to those nearby regions light could traverse—all else remains forever beyond our reach. At both extremes, it seemed, the universe had been created unknowable, the manifestation of some irreducible mystery that could be as well expressed by the poet as by the physicist.

But of course the new description was successful, my friend. That is the nature of science—it works. When it doesn't we discard it for something that works better. As a scientist one cannot afford to become sentimental about any particular depiction of reality. In the final analysis it did not matter how much I wanted to believe in the old order. The new science cleared up the discrepancy in Mercury's orbit, escaped the dilemma of things standing still or moving infinitely fast, and dispensed utterly with any need for God's throne. And what has given us the bomb has also caused that garden of lights to bloom in the desert—and all the other products of our world that we take for granted and would not wish to do without. We cannot escape them. Few of us would even consider it.

But what is a triumph of human ingenuity is not necessarily a victory of the will. I realized it didn't matter whether the new physics was strange and foreign to our way of perceiving reality, or how well it worked. What mattered was that there were new mysteries; that the success of the new ideas in clearing up the old mysteries brought with them more unanswerable questions; that even if we replaced the new description with another more satisfying one—as eventually we must—we would still be left with some other set of questions; that any attempt to know what was humanly unknowable, because we are either too small or too large to experience it for ourselves, would leave us in mystery; and that this process is a never-ending one.

There will always be mystery, my friend, no matter what success we may find in manipulating nature for our own ends. For the first time, I think, I understood what the artist was trying to say and why I had not understood it before. I no longer felt alienated but strangely akin to what I once wanted to discount as meaningless and irrelevant. My reality became not one but a manifold of equally valid realities to be explored; and I would never again be able to take any of them for granted.

Should I have been surprised? No, of course not, my friend. What I faced were merely the unanswerable questions of the philosopher in another guise. What could not be answered before could not be answered now—and will not be answered ever. If there is any mystery, then it is all a mystery. What I had at last realized was nothing more than the acceptance expressed in the wonder of a child, or that sense of the absurd that can strike any of us at any moment. I had not suffered the disillusionment of the loss of certainty. I had instead found a reason—the only valid and changeless reason—for continuing. There is a wonder to it; and it is not merely the innocence of a child but the wonder and amazement of you and me, as we sit here looking out at the mystery blazing before us in the night—if we but take the time.

If we ever truly understood, we would be through, my friend—finished. We might experience some existence but it would not be this one. If we could hold all of this in our minds, it would be nothing. We don't really want to know; each of us understands that. We, like the philosophers, only want to hold on to the tantalizing hope that somehow it might be possible. But if it were, I think we would quickly perish as a biological phenomenon—consciousness with no need to contemplate would become superfluous in the scheme of things—and be replaced by some simpler, more vital force that could partake blindly of the mystery, the way everything does now in perfect harmony. We would become God, who having created the universe is left with no further purpose, and dies.

I have sat here some nights, when there was nothing else to do, until dawn and watched those pin pricks of light down there, one by one, wink out, disappear into the light of day, the way the evening before they had appeared out of it—day giving way to night and night in turn to day, without end. We are only the latest. Before us, there were the campfires of countless tribes and wandering bands who walked this valley and these slopes as far back as there were humans here to do so. We tell ourselves there is a certainty to it. But in truth it is the lack of certainty that keeps us going. The curiosity about how it will all turn out; the hanging on till the last possible moment to see how it unfolds, to take one more chance on finally learning the truth.

There is no certainty—beyond our apprehension of the uncertain. We would have given up long ago, except for that. How much happier I am now, my friend, not ever being able to know the truth.

4

Greetings again, my friend; pull up a chair and join me. You are just in time too. Your drink is fresh; it only just arrived. The first drink of the evening is always the most pleasurable, don't you agree? It is the one that lets us shed the cares of the day and drop our guard and become receptive to bold thoughts, while still holding on to the critical acumen that allows us to judge them fairly. Let us use the time to reflect on what we have said.

I was somewhat curious after last evening to see whether you would return. I am pleased, and reassured, that you have not given up. My story, I confess, took a rather unexpected turn. For me, at the time, it was likewise an eye opening realization; but it is one that everyone has to get past at some point. But what is there left, you ask, after the loss of all certainty? Why simply everything, my friend. Only certainty is limiting. I am afraid that you may be confusing certainty with hope. One is an intellectual recognition; the other merely a mental attitude. The loss of certainty is not inconsistent with hope. Our only real hope, my friend, lies in understanding that nothing in this world, or this life, is ever certain.

No, I didn't simply surrender at that point, my friend. Nor did I become resigned. Admittedly, what I revealed to you in our conversation last evening marked a definite turning point in my thinking. Things were never to be the same again. But I kept going through the motions for a long time afterwards. I admit the dream was gone—the tidy little world of my own where I would spend my time isolated in the assurance of everything that happened; where I would be able to understand it all and have no need of anything outside of that reassuring faith in the predictable and well-ordered functioning of immutable natural law—but there had been disappointments before, and many others since.

How many shattered dreams do you see in the eyes of our companions? Look around you. Over there is one who dreamed of being rich only to lose everything he held dear in the process. With him is another who bartered everything on the prospect of fame and adulation, but now consoles himself by associating with those he believes are even greater failures, to regain his self-respect. There are others here this evening, outwardly merry to mask their inner disappointments, whose similar stories are written in their eyes. One detects them in unguarded moments when someone has had too much to drink or thinks no one notices, or they slip out in a revealing phrase in innocent conversation, but always the signs are there. Life is a succession of failed dreams, each one shaping the next, until finally there is nothing left to hope for, or the will fails, and we give up. I could have said that man is a dreamer, rather than a creature of reflection, but it is the same thing. We regard our situation and dream the next dream, the one we hope will come true and wipe out the memory of all the ones that disappointed us before. But that is only a kind of false hope.

You think I am only being cynical? I suppose the truth always contains an element of what we label as cynicism. Are there dreams that come true, my friend, or is it that we have not really dreamed? Of course it may happen, but I am speaking of those more numerous and less fortunate who in their disappointment are like us in our peril. Out there somewhere at this very moment the companion of a deserted woman, herself concerned only about where the next meal will come from, is beating her child out of the frustrations of his own failure. Yet tomorrow each of them in their own way will reformulate the dream, and go on dreaming of the next time, and the next, always in hopes of something better. My disappointments were minor by comparison.

I finished my studies and received my degree. For a while I even continued the pursuit of basic research, those investigations with no purpose beyond revealing nature's secrets. I discovered a number of small but fundamental phenomena. Nothing of any great consequence or important enough to be named after me, yet significant enough to stamp me as an individual of promise and to open new doors. Those who had given me my degree felt vindicated. Those with whom I worked looked upon me with a respect that was gratifying and provided me great latitude. I accepted the praise and the opportunities it afforded. At times I found myself wanting to believe they were right in their assessment of me, but privately I knew otherwise. I better than anyone realized how inconsiderable were my accomplishments when compared to what I had set out to do. I had been simply lucky—stumbled onto some relatively inconsequential details that others had overlooked, but which were a far cry from true understanding. The belief in certainty had vanished; I realized now it was impossible.

I no longer looked upon the knowledge I had acquired as the key to unlocking the secrets of the universe. Instead I came to see it for what it is: a body of *technique* by which we manipulate our situation to our own ends. A tool, no different from all the other tools we have devised for ourselves. No more or less useful in revealing the meaning of reality than a wheel or a socket wrench. I turned from being a *scientist*, my friend, to becoming the consummate *technician*.

I still called myself a scientist. It was to my benefit to do so. The public is in awe of what it doesn't understand and perceives so much reason to mistrust. Yet it was not the cause of science that interested me but what I could use it to do—for myself as much as for others. I mentioned that I had learned to get along, that I had become adaptable, even manipulative, in my affairs. And now I found that I also possessed considerable power—power rooted in my skill at manipulating people, in the knowledge I possessed that they didn't, and in my willingness to use both for my own purposes. I told myself that I had the common welfare at heart—it is not natural to regard oneself unfavorably—but my actions spoke louder. It was selfishness that guided my behavior.

Does that sound overly harsh? I don't intend that it should. It is natural that we behave so. It would be foolish to expect otherwise. We have survived this long by looking out for ourselves, why should anyone think we would suddenly change just because our actions can set off megaton bombs or foul the environment or spread a virus? Those things may or may not happen, no one knows for certain, but at this instant our actions are justifiable for any number of other reasons, most of them in harmony with our immediate welfare.

I am not condemning myself, merely trying to be faithful to the truth as I perceive it. Clearly I am no more at fault than those who do what they believe they must to get through the day, never intending harm to themselves or others even if it comes to that. We could all be wrong, but no action is so simple as to be truly understandable. I see that you smoke, my friend, and I dare say that both of us drink a bit more than we should, but who is to say? As someone has noted: the first cigarette in the morning, the last glass of wine at evening—those who believe they will convince us to give them up by telling us the probabilities are the mistaken ones. It is all a gamble anyway.

Slowly I was corrupted into believing that my interests and the common welfare were one and the same. Perhaps it is necessary in order to live with oneself; or perhaps one does indeed come to believe it without question after a time. More likely it is easier not to think about it at all.

At any rate I didn't think about it, except in a certain arrogant fashion that made it unthinkable I might be wrong. By now I had an enormous investment in what I did. I was trained for it, I was extremely good at it, and I enjoyed it immensely. With it I had achieved success and respect and financial security. I was a member of the establishment. People extended me the benefit of the doubt; my failings were overlooked, or excused. I could do no wrong. It was a privilege that it was only necessary not to abuse, and once granted, success was assured. My efforts also supported others who were dependent on what I did. My actions were not only *justified*, they had become *indispensable* as well.

I became corrupted in other ways, too. I began to *believe* in what I was doing. I invented things—established a reputation as a clever person. Once I had invented something, I considered that everyone should automatically desire it, as the solution to whatever problem—however insignificant—had led to its conception. I peddled my inventions and my ideas. I became incredulous, and exasperated, whenever anyone suggested that my latest invention was not necessary after all, that others would be perfectly content to do without it. I deemed that no problem should go uncorrected for which some new technological trinket could be the *ideal* solution.

I viewed every situation in terms of how it could be addressed by the use of more, or better, technology—*better* always in the sense of more sophisticated and challenging. Simple solutions began to lose their appeal. They didn't require the skills I had acquired and for which I was paid so handsomely for doing what I enjoyed doing anyway. I lost sympathy with those who were fearful or distrustful of technological fixes. They were living in the past, in the midst of a present that clearly pointed toward a tomorrow based on technology. It was our destiny, and I counted myself among its chosen representatives.

I imagined a gleaming future in which no problem was beyond the reach of technology. Those that might be would remain so only while the technology caught up, in what was an unending and ever accelerating process that would make possible within a very short span feats so advanced that they were at present unimaginable. There were no limits. Whatever appeared limited was just the consequence of our imperfect knowledge and would be remedied in time. Hadn't that always proved true? To imagine any end to it was to make the same mistake as those who said man would never fly or set foot on the moon. The problems we faced were not warnings of a perilous future but were temporary challenges to our continued progress. Challenges to be met and overcome by the same approach that had gotten us this far.

My youthful propensity for dreaming returned, and I liked nothing better than to sit for hours imagining solutions to imagined problems. Rather than feeling apprehensive at the suggestion of some possible calamity in the making, I became gleeful at the prospects of another problem whose solution would demonstrate again the triumph of technology over any obstacle. My particular fancy lay in addressing situations that others attributed to the misuse of technology. Things like pollution of the environment and global warming, depletion of the ozone layer, overpopulation; and all those disasters that could be imagined as a consequence of natural forces at work—volcanoes and earthquakes, the weather, the next ice age, collision with a comet. I would carefully construct in my mind potential fixes, then imagine every conceivable problem that each of them in turn could lead to, and then construct solutions to those too, and on and on, like tracing all the possible steps in an imaginary game of chess played against fate.

During these tranquil hours of pleasant diversion the need for proper management was driven home to me. I could not imagine remedies that did not require the most careful and attentive implementation to have any chance of being successful. These situations were far too complex, and too crucial to our welfare, to be left to the whims of whatever "natural" happenings were normally responsible for their outcome. If natural processes had been sufficient in the first place, we wouldn't be in the predicament we faced. It was only necessary to understand a process first, in order to alter it or replace it by one more beneficial to us. Natural order might be sufficient for the workings of nature, but the human intellect transcended nature and made anything possible. And where anything was possible, and such great works conceivable for the benefit of humanity, my friend had been right: one had a responsibility not to sit idly by and do nothing. It was not only what I *enjoyed* doing, it was my *moral duty* as well.

Against the force of such conviction there was simply no argument. I shunned any thought of being wrong. I dismissed the past as a series of amusing and naive blunders. I became a confirmed futurist.

Antiques and anything old became abhorrent to me. I preferred modern furniture and new buildings, glass and steel and concrete, synthetic fibers and plastic impregnated woods. I judged everything by whether it looked old-fashioned or modern. No craftsman, no artisan could fabricate with the precision and consistency of a machine, preferably one fully automated and immune to human variance. What was made by hand was inexact and inefficient and undesirable. Museums I avoided unless there were displays of modern technology—I detested abstract art and sculpture as meaningless, and a useless waste of effort— or if I attended it was to gloat with a sense of superiority at the lack of sophistication of other cultures and other times.

The present constantly disappointed and frustrated me. I gauged everything not by current standards but by what I imagined possible in the future, and I was anxious to have it at hand. In my desire to hasten the inevitable I gave no thought to my own mortality. If I thought of death at all it was only in terms of a general regret at not being able to see what wonders lay in store for us. I solaced myself with the conviction that the future was assured, and that I knew in what direction it was headed.

Little by little I withdrew into an existence based almost entirely on our own creations. My evenings were spent watching television. Every concept I had of the outside world was either derived from, or gradually replaced by, what I saw on TV. Or I watched video movies, or played the latest video games on my home computer. If I ventured out in the evenings it was to visit the shopping malls and wander about, examining the newest products. I spent my weekends the same way. I confined my reading to technical material and an occasional work of science fiction. On vacation I traveled to cities, picking out the most modern for my itinerary and booking flights on the latest and most advanced aircraft. Whenever I did get into the countryside it was to visit a dam or power station or some other miracle of human engineering. I liked nothing better than to go on tours of manufacturing facilities, to see the complex and sophisticated processes by which some intricate product was produced.

In my arrogance I scorned those whose situation identified them as disadvantaged—inferior is a term I would have used without hesitation. Their plight was their own fault. There were solutions at hand—there were always solutions to any problem—and one had only to implement them and correct the situation. Failure to do so counted as a failure of will, a sign of moral weakness and decay, and a tacit admission of inferiority. I accepted no excuses or reasons on their behalf. Circumstances were never beyond our control. Some people just gave up too easily. To admit otherwise would have cast doubt on all I espoused. I had learned to avert my eyes whenever what I saw was not what I had expected, or wanted, to see.

Thus, my friend, did I eventually become that curious mixture of *Homo sciens*, *Homo faber* and *Homo ministerium* that I earlier termed the *scientist-technician*.

Naturally, with such leanings, I would pursue a career in a setting where these inclinations could find full expression. Not every opportunity afforded the grand scale on which I imagined doing things. Of course there were corporations engaged in projects that I found enticing, but generally the corporate mind thought too small or there was the hindrance of having to show a profit. None could afford to plunge into undertakings that were challenging or grandiose enough to satisfy my sense of importance. I wanted to have my finger on the technical pulse of our destiny, to attempt something of such magnitude that it would be pivotal in shaping the future. Nothing less was worthy of the energy and ambition I was willing to dedicate to the task.

I would have to look to those institutions funded by public monies—let society underwrite my technical ambitions. I sought undertakings determined not by any considerations of profit or financial return, or even of the public welfare, but by what funds could be wheedled from a gullible and fearful public by manipulative politicians and the military and those like myself whose special interests were served. The opportunities abounded.

Weapons, you are thinking. Not just *any* weapons, my friend. By what I did next I revealed the true extent of my arrogance and disdain. I chose to work on the bomb.

And I did it here, in the very desert that had been its birthplace.

Where men of similar arrogance and curiosity and dedication before me had wrested the secrets of its cosmic fires from that symboled language of beauty that adorned my wall. By those who knew in the triumph of their labors the corruption of power and ego, betraying soul and conscience for the sweeter taste of discovery. And yet, who were innocent of any act but what eventually would have been done by someone, somewhere. That is, by those who only behaved thoroughly humanly.

Does my confession surprise you? Of course not, you are a practical man. These days we are resigned to the fact of the bomb. I might even have said comfortable with it for the most part. We do not want to surrender it ourselves, but only to have everyone else do so. It is just one more out of all the calamities imaginable.

The number of them is enough to assure that we do not become too distressed by any one at a time. In a world of specialization each potential disaster has its host of loyal followers, ready to trundle out their favorite cause and hold it up to the public consciousness whenever it serves their particular interests—to be met by the outcry of all those who feel their own interests threatened.

It is impossible to take it all seriously and go on living with any sense of purpose. I do not mean to suggest that we can dismiss it altogether. Crises come and go, and business in this establishment has never been better. It would be just as foolish to ignore our plight as to be intimidated by it. Prudence dictates that one be aware of circumstances, but who among us trusts the power of the individual to affect the outcome? I mean, my friend, the ability of a single person obeying the voice of conscience to have any impact on the course of events?

After all, why should it be surprising that I chose to work on the bomb? I merely did what each of us has done, what we are doing still. What we have always done and will keep on doing for as long as we have the chance. Our peril is not the product of a few misguided people; it is the result of everything we do, all of us together. Each of us participates in his own way. Some to greater effect than others, but the final outcome is the sum of all the individual acts that fit together to form the mosaic of this panorama in which we are collectively engaged.

Can we judge the contribution of a single act, or the consequence of refusing to behave in any particular manner? All we can know with certainty is what happens, and all of us must bear a share of the responsibility for our role in the outcome. Death is the only absolution possible, my friend. Barring that, the living are accountable.

The bomb—and I speak of it only as an example—is not the product of a few specially endowed individuals who were able to achieve what no one else could have. That is part of the myth that surrounds these things. The bomb was not the product of genius, but of nature itself. Many quite ordinary people like you and me working together have made it, my friend, and brought it to the present state of perfection in killing people. Politicians, the military, educators, businessmen, clerks, housewives—all were necessary in addition to those who first conceived it and in whose imagination it took shape, in order that we could have arrived at the point where we stand today.

And if it goes off its light will shine alike on all those who, without even the least understanding of its workings, labored for its fulfillment and participated in whatever small way to make it possible. No one will be justified in standing apart and crying, "I told you so," though doubtless many will react that way. It is not so simple to purchase one's innocence in a world of such complexity and mystery, where evil remains a constant possibility.

You see, no one is in charge, my friend. Unless some*one* is responsible, everyone is. Do not speak to me about degrees of responsibility. Those are merely categories we create for ourselves in order to pass judgment on others. There is only responsibility: that which each of us incurs by drawing breath and choosing to live; by continuing to struggle to survive and to strive and hope and aspire and dream and do all those things that uniquely determine us.

I know what you are thinking. You are about to accuse me of moral relativism, of arguing that if everyone is guilty then no one is, of using that as a reason to justify any behavior. I am not talking about choices. That is another matter entirely. Of course we must choose. Every action entails a choice. Doing nothing is itself a choice. I am only interested in what happens to us as a result, and whether or not we are guilty or innocent together; whether by claiming to be innocent we can escape our involvement in this human experience.

Far from justifying my behavior, it was instead the realization that made me decide—choose, if you will—to have nothing more to do with this enterprise. For it convinced me that we would indeed use these weapons. It is merely a matter of time and circumstances. When no one is in charge and so many are involved, things have a way of happening that no one intended, yet they happen. We behave socially. Some look upon it as a virtue of ours. But in effect it may only mean that we behave in ways no one is able to anticipate or control in any sort of predictable fashion; that we are acting out this human drama in blind obedience to some impulse we can as yet only hint at for all our supposed understanding and knowledge.

The bomb will be used again, if only because we do not act as if we believed otherwise; and again and again, until we begin to behave in some fashion that would prevent it. No one knows when or where or how but that is unimportant. What matters is that we continue to take each of the small steps that in the end will make it possible, until at some point it will become inevitable. The weapons are there, the situation arises, someone will deem it appropriate, others will agree, and it will happen; just as it has so many times before and will countless times again. Once we gained this new tool we were doomed to keep using it. It isn't the tools that kill, it is us; and constraint is not to be found in weapons, whether of greater or lesser destructiveness. We devised them to destroy; why show surprise when that is how we use them, even when our own destruction is threatened in return?

All our peril is of the same sort, my friend. What is true of the bomb is true of every hazard we face. No one seems to want it to happen but the danger keeps on mounting nonetheless. It is part of the mystery, along with whether we are in control of anything or whether we merely believe we are in order to keep going, to find a reason to hope for a possible future. It will be taken care of by something, but perhaps something beyond our control, something of which we are only an insignificant part. Maybe it is best that we don't know. Complacency or resignation might become substitutes for action.

The bomb will be used. When we created it, it took its place along with us in the world. The transfixing roar of its doom will sound like only a more deafening thunderclap, yet every bit as natural as the ones accompanying those flashes of lightning off there in the distance. That it did not occur before we made it does not make it any less natural. Nature made it possible, and we, all of us together, brought it to fruition. If we are destroyed in the process, or some of us are, then the toll will stand alongside that of all the other natural calamities in our world. It is our possession now. It belongs to us—to those who are touched by it and who are part of this civilization that created it—and for whom its use is a constant threat. It and all the dangers we face are not accidents. They are the natural consequence of our collective actions. They are deeply rooted in our nature.

The bomb will be used again, my friend; the dangers will be with us always. Once I realized it, I felt a great sense of relief, and I ceased to worry about it any further.

5

You are later than usual this evening, my worthy colleague. No matter; you are here at last, and welcome. I am afraid that drink is spoiled by now. Just set it aside. He will promptly bring us a fresh round. I took the liberty of ordering your usual for both of us.

I am truly glad to see you. I have grown quite fond of our evenings together. I had almost begun to be concerned that, after what I revealed about myself last evening, you had decided to relinquish your Distinguished Chair of the Philosophy of Life as It Should Be in disgust and join the ranks of those others before you. I should have deeply regretted that, my friend. I can honestly say that no more perceptive or stimulating adversary has occupied that chair.

Then I could understand if, after last evening, you thought there was nothing left for me to reveal. I should have regretted that most of all, my friend. For the revelations of last evening do not mark the end of my story, but only its beginning. If my story stopped there, I would not be here talking with you, for I would have little to say.

Yes, of course, my realization was sobering, but also personally liberating. It freed me to be concerned about more important things. After that I had no desire to be personally involved; it had come to seem like a foolish endeavor. That is, my friend, I did not wish to do anything myself directly to contribute. Otherwise I continued to behave in much the same manner. I still paid my taxes, and those who regularly voted funds for more weapons counted on my support at election time. I numbered among my best friends many who were engaged in my former profession. And I remained a member in good standing of a society committed to a course of action that I believed foolish and dangerous—even pointless, if anything so much a part of nature can be spoken of in those terms.

I still went to the same places, did the same things. My preoccupations remained as before. For a brief time I even pondered ways to counter the threat by the clever use of technology. But at length I was forced to admit that I had met my match. Try as I might to imagine a solution, I encountered at every turn the stark realization that machines and implements were powerless against a determined and ruthless adversary. I saw how the most intricate and ingenious schemes imaginable could be thwarted by the simplest and most straightforward of remedies. More direct approaches worked no better. Nothing was of any use.

It seemed the only realistic way to counter being destroyed was to threaten to destroy everything in return. That option, if implemented, brought about the very situation it was designed to avoid. There were other ruses not beyond imagining, but somehow they did not seem real anymore, like laws intended to banish murder by merely declaring it a crime and fixing a punishment. No threatened severity is ever sufficient to deter nature. By now my heart was not in it.

All of the myriad dangers confronting us took on the same aspect. Together they loomed before me like the unanswerable questions of the philosophers. By comparison our solutions seemed like so much meaningless and ineffectual babble. I realized that if there was even a single problem that technology could not counter, then there would be others. And if there were any, their number would be limitless. That is the distinction, my friend, so easily overlooked by these scientist-technicians. They believe instead that the technological possibilities are endless. To them one triumph means that any triumph is possible. The bomb goes off—because the laws of physics allow it—and they believe afterward that it can just as easily be made not to, all at their bidding. They wish to ignore that what God has permitted, man cannot forbid.

Deep down I felt a growing uneasiness, a nagging apprehension. I was plagued by doubts. This world I had created assumed the aspect of something synthetic and artificial, something that could be twisted and broken and shattered beyond repair, like the plastic and metal and glass out of which it was fashioned. I began to be aware of its frailty, and I felt less and less sure of myself.

Then one day, without warning, the clocks in my world stopped. First one, then one by one, all of them together, utterly ceased. That in itself might not have been portentous. By my reaction to it, however, I shaped its significance: I became oblivious to time, yet never more acutely aware of it. The mechanical ticking of the escapement was replaced by the reassuring beat of my own heart; the current in an electric motor by the vital flow of electrical pulses of nervous energy.

How strange to see those hands standing so motionless, yet have life go on the same. What is to be done, my friend, when all of one's dreams have at last failed? Why that is just the point at which life truly begins. Everything enduring rises like the phoenix from the ashes of some earlier failure.

It began quite innocently. A casual glance at my wristwatch first roused my suspicion. When I put it to my ear the pure concert A tone of its tiny tuning fork no longer hummed the cadence of time in perfect pitch. I pressed it harder against my ear but all I felt was a cold empty silence. I listened intently for a long time, thinking perhaps I would hear it still. What I heard were just my own thoughts.

No, I didn't think of a dead battery or of replacing the watch with a new one, or of anything having to do with cause and effect. I thought instead of that awful, scary silence roaring in my ears, deafening me with its emptiness, like the sound of the ocean echoing inside an empty sea shell. I kept waiting for it to be filled up again with the clear, unbroken strain of that 440 cycle-per-second symphony of time. Often I had pressed the smooth glass crystal to my ear just to hear its reaffirming note reminding me that all was well. Now it was permanently drowned out in the blaring of my thoughts, and they, broken and jumbled, were chaotic. They rushed onward, erratically, one after another in an unending staccato stream like a clock marking some unpredictable progression of time to an ever changing beat. I listened, fascinated by the sounds of silence, by the possibility—and the threat—of nothingness that this moment afforded.

But there was no void; my thoughts quickly filled it and the moment passed. In the silence time did not stand still. Only now it set its own tempo, marked not by the steady hum of a tuning fork but by the faltering pace of consciousness; by an internal awareness of a truer time which took its cues from the mind that regarded it. It was not my thoughts that I was most aware of, but the act of thinking: a stony, impassive contemplation of consciousness. There was no void, no nothingness; only consciousness aware of itself.

Then somewhere in that silence I heard my own pulse, pounding in my ear. Faintly at first, then louder and louder, until it obscured every other sensation, every thought. I took the watch away and the pounding continued. The repetitive, predictable cadence was calming, reassuring.

Gently I placed the tips of my fingers against my wrist, and then my neck, and felt the rhythmic pulsing of blood flowing through my veins. At that moment I had my fingers on the beating heart of the universe, on the vital force that fuels the engine of this vast machine.

No, my friend, not a machine—the very opposite—but it is a metaphor I use intentionally. We have tried in vain to reduce it all to a grand mechanism functioning according to a few simple principles. It is amazing how well the analogy works. With it we can cook our meals and explore the atom and the cosmos. But, for all that, we cannot find nourishment adequate to our needs, or discover that for which we seem to be searching.

This quest of ours is a relatively recent undertaking and one already advanced beyond our dreams. The twinkling lights stretching across the mesa and up and down the valley are among the brightest jewels in its crown. Even the bomb fills us with a secret envy. If we were to look long enough we could find among all these other pin pricks of light in the sky the glow of a man-made moon circling the earth, and be reminded of photographs taken of Martian landscapes and the barren moons of other planets. And it is only just beginning. It will continue unabated to wherever it is leading us; there is no turning back. These first few milestones are but confusing markers along the way.

Still, at that moment when I felt my pulse and heard the pounding in my ears, I was acutely aware that it is not a machine but something much more mysterious. Something for which there will be no analogy, no metaphor, no way of understanding beyond reaching out to touch it. To hold it in one's hand and listen to its heartbeat. To see and smell and taste it—like a child. For compared to the enormity of the task we are all children.

I put the watch on my dresser. The numbers on its face seemed irrelevant and no longer held my interest. No, I wasn't suddenly set adrift. That first evening the sun went down at the anticipated time. I awoke the next morning at the usual hour, took about the same time to dress for work, and arrived in step with everyone else. I conducted my affairs the same as before. Occasionally I would be late for meetings or other appointments, but that only served to emphasize my presence, and rather than any inconvenience, actually worked to my advantage.

By my tardiness I took control, where before I had been the pawn of others. I was made to appear busy, even overworked, someone who was greatly in demand and vitally involved. I was sought out by those who previously paid me no attention. By asking for clarification, or to have some point I had missed repeated, I could interject myself at meetings and take charge of the discussions. On the other hand, arriving late, I could sit back and assess what was going on before deciding whether I wished to be involved, then blame a busy schedule already too full of commitments whenever I didn't. I avoided the meaningless small talk and social posturing which invariably begin meetings. Scurrying away already late for my next appointment, I brought them to a crisp conclusion. Some I managed to avoid altogether by arriving after they were finished.

Soon afterwards I had the wall clock in my office removed too, and gained an additional measure of independence. Then one day the radio in my car failed. I could no longer listen to the correct time, or to the news reports that had punctuated the drive to and from work. Rather than having it repaired, I left it silent. I listened instead to the wind whistling past the windows and to the sounds of traffic. The world outside my view and beyond my hearing went on the same whether or not I was aware of it, and the drive was not noticeably longer or briefer.

What can be said of our time, my friend? Just that we listened to the news. Not that we read the newspapers—that dates us. In an age of information, reading is too inefficient and has become outmoded. By the time anything can be written it is part of the past, and there is nothing anymore of such permanence that it merits reflection. We have moved on beyond that—to an oral tradition again: our bards are the newscasters who tell us of the day's events. They speak to us from anywhere on earth, or from the surface of the moon and the planets. Homer never sounded sweeter, and he did not have necessity on his side.

Still, if anything, I became even more conscious of time. I began to watch the sunset. Not as a spectacle of astonishing beauty—I had hardly ever noticed it before; and certainly I had not been overwhelmed by its splendor—but as an event that marked a turning point in each day, part of the natural passage of time. As I sat on my balcony at dusk I would watch the first faint glimmer of stars in the paling sky, and the city lights, as one by one they winked on, until the darkened surface of the earth and the black sky overhead were a studded glow. I learned to recognize Jupiter and Venus, Mars and Saturn, and to follow their changing patterns in the night sky as they wandered back and forth across the heavens in their journeys about the sun. Soon I could identify Orion with his belt and sword, the dog star Sirius, the twins Castor and Pollux, the chair of Cassiopeia. Then Leo and the Scorpion, Cygnus the swan, the winged horse Pegasus, and Deneb, Vega, Arcturus and Capella. With them I learned to tell time in the night sky and to follow the progression of seasons from spring to winter.

No, of course I could not have learned to do so as readily, nor as quickly, without those clocks that for me had stopped ticking—or without the knowledge they signify. I have not meant to deny that other world, my friend, merely to declare some measure of independence. Neither had I any intention of accepting it as the only reality. I was fortunate that I lived in the desert, where the night sky blazes bright and clear and where one need only look around to discover that other reality.

I arose before dawn to observe the constellations, those just rising and those setting, and to watch the sunrise count down the beginning of a new day. I discovered the symmetry of dawn and dusk: that the seasons and time can be read in the patterns of the stars as well at either moment. Neither one marks a beginning or an end but both at once: an event, a ticking of time that signals the end of day and the beginning of night and back again, in an endless succession that is the one true clock. The primordial clock of the universe is not a machine based on some simple principle but the heartbeat of an unfathomable mystery, linking us to all the other mysteries around us in which we recognize the same beating heart, feel the same palpable pulse.

At dawn the songs of the passerines marked the time between first light and the rising of the sun, and later heralded the arrival of morning. The changing nuances of light on the mesas and on the rock faces of the mountains measured the progress of the day, and the shadows told time as they always have. Noon has a look and a feel to it that changes with the seasons, but each is unmistakable and requires no clock, indicating both time and season in a single impression. Past noon, events reversed; shadows lengthened and shades of light deepened from shimmering to more subtle. At the appointed time the chorus of bird songs signaled the approach of late afternoon, the way it had announced the arrival of morning, then ushered in the sunset, and dusk, and finally the cloak of darkness in the haunting flute tones of the thrushes.

It was superfluous to check these events against any timepiece made by man. Rather the timepiece should be validated against them, as the one is but an imitation of the other, the way logic is but a semblance of reason. There is a time that has no need of us, that beats silently in the rhythm of events and that would beat as surely and with the same rhythm whether we were here to witness it or not. It has no need of us—but we have every need of it. For our existence hangs precariously by the slender thread of its swinging pendulum. We owe our being to whatever faint heartbeat reverberates through this cosmic chain of events, against which we are but a meaningless, insignificant perturbation.

I had not sensed it in the form of consciousness aware of itself, but in the throbbing of its mystery—in the motion of an amoeba, the struggle of a hatchling to break free of the egg, the explosion of a super nova. There is no universal consciousness, my friend. To think so would be to make the whole like the least significant of its parts, to ascribe a meaning to all of this that is unwarranted except as an attempt at self-aggrandizement and some grand self-delusion. There is only being and mystery—and whatever meaning we choose to give them. I have not changed my mind about that. Nor have I contradicted what I said earlier. We can comprehend our insignificance and still be assured of our importance. The two are not contradictory; they are the same thing.

Then one morning when I looked in the mirror I saw stamped on my features the only clock that matters, and it told me how late the hour had grown. At some point life is suddenly half over and we begin to notice all the little changes that have gradually accumulated. Lines creased the corners of my eyes and framed my mouth. An old scar on my chin had become prominent. Deep furrows cut across my forehead when I frowned, and my countenance had grown rather stern and hard. Gone was the pleasant, exuberant mask of youth. In its place stared back a more serious face, one with a wiser but sadder mien. Could this be me, I puzzled? I read in those features an admission of the turn my thoughts had taken.

Can we read faces, my friend? Are they mirrors—windows on the soul—or masks of what they hide from others, even from ourselves? There is a poetry of faces, and as with poems one may choose to lie or not. Yet could anyone doubt the honesty of a child's wide-eyed innocence? Still less, the face I saw in that mirror.

Its eyes met mine with an openness that concealed nothing. Behind them I saw a soul in need of confession, in possession of truths it had not dared to admit but could no longer deny or escape. They were serious eyes, piercing and intense, but if one peered more deeply there was also in them a yearning that betrayed a look of anguish. I was staring into the soul of one who had come to some great realization that was both reassuring and threatening. There was the tranquility and resignation of truth, but of a truth more serious and demanding than any faced before, one that would never subside.

I forced a smile. The features softened, but portrayed a lie, and quickly lapsed back to the more serious aspect of the moment before. Yes, this was the face of truth. The likeness was certainly mine, and what I read in my eyes was ineluctable.

Transported to that final realization of some great truth—who can ever explain it, my friend? We simply know it, with a clarity and a lucidity that is its own proof. We know it and we cannot go beyond that. Any attempt at logic is futile by comparison. What need have we of what only appears to be logical? We have been deceived repeatedly—whether the universe is finite or not, whether it had a beginning or will ever end, whether there is a God—the list is endless and any child can extend it. The unanswerable *why* of our most youthful innocence.

Then comes the moment when at last we are certain. The difference, once experienced, is never forgotten. Logic—reason—can be dismissed with a knowing smile. This other is undeniable, and the source of an ineffable joy. Even the most terrible truths, once revealed, cease to be threatening. We can fear only what we are free to doubt. The knowledge of one's death? No, it is still too abstract. We are speaking here of the *realization* at the instant of death. That is the sort of truth I had discovered.

Yet do we act on our truths, my friend? That is another matter. We might argue that our species is quite naturally schizophrenic. The schisms dividing us are as numerous and as complex as our situation. I have already confessed that at some point I had no wish to continue my former profession. What I said was true enough. Yet for a long time I carried on as before. It was much later that I actually quit. In between I was living a lie—or rather two lies—for I harbored and professed one belief but behaved just the opposite.

Which of us finds it possible to act strictly in accordance with our convictions? To insist on it only brings harm to others for the sake of an empty principle. Beware of those who claim to; they are either charlatans or madmen. More likely they think it possible because they are ignorant, or because they do not have any real principles except those that can be adjusted to fit the situation. I am afraid the conclusion is unavoidable.

We are all a bit schizoid. In each of us there is a principled person who must continually compromise out of the necessity to act. Sometimes for the better, sometimes for the worse—but that is irrelevant.

I mentioned earlier that one must get along. Perhaps it means that one ends up behaving as necessity requires, when what was intended was either much better or far worse—it can go either way. Yet we are forced to act if we do not wish to sacrifice ourselves. I am not speaking of martyrdom; that is always possible. The rest of us behave as moral schizophrenics, denying the basis of our actions by submerging them in a corrupt set of beliefs. We cannot escape though. We confess our true beliefs in the pragmatism of our actions. Yes, actions do speak louder than words. Before there was language there was the behavior that gave rise to it, even, I dare say, social behavior engendered by the same impulses that still bind us together. It makes no sense to separate words and actions into individual categories. Separate from actions the words are meaningless anyway. All that matters is that we are presented with choices, and we must finally choose. We may wish not to reveal ourselves, only to be betrayed by our actions. Not only by whether or not we choose, but by what we choose.

I recall my own youthful impulse to remain apart, separate from the fray, a detached observer of the human condition. To such a one actions would be everything, for they would be the only thing. Even without the endless rationalization that accompanies them, such an observer would know our true choices by observing our actions. To him language would add nothing. Without it he would not suffer the same confusion and uncertainty we reveal in our self-serving rhetoric. He would merely observe and catalog, like a physicist describing the behavior of electrons. And our real ethics would be written in that catalog of our behavior.

Who knows why I chose to remain on for so long? Timidity, cowardice, expediency, greed, power, status, ego? Those are just words; in this case empty sounds. My actions explain it all: I simply remained. Whatever else I might have believed, or professed, was subservient to that fact.

Must we live a lie then? Only if we choose to deny our actions, my friend. Yet most of us will find it necessary at some point.

6

Welcome once more, my friend. Please, sit down and relax for a while. Let the cares and trials of the day gradually subside with the slow setting of the sun. I have chosen our places for the evening with that particular enjoyment in mind. We are in store for yet another of the spectacular sunsets that endear me to this place and keep me here. I know I will witness only so many in the time I have remaining, and I should not like to miss even a single one.

Our drinks will be here momentarily. Ah, there, he is coming now. Such selfless attention. What a dedicated and conscientious servant. It is through the efforts, and the willingness, of ones like him that the world functions at all, and we, my friend, and others like us who enjoy our little privileges are forever in their debt. We should never forget it for an instant.

My story depends on it far more than I have acknowledged, but one cannot properly credit everything that has brought us to this moment or we would never get beyond the prologue. I know it may sound like everything is always about me, but I don't mean it that way, I assure you. It is about him too, and all like him, as he shuffles back and forth among these tables fulfilling the desires and wishes of those he so faithfully serves. Those who, in their exalted view, think his fortunes depend directly on them, in reality are far more dependent on him.

Privilege, my friend. How few of us really comprehend it. Most of us mistakenly believe we got here largely by our own efforts. It is natural, I suppose, to congratulate ourselves and take too much pride in our meager accomplishments. Yet few of us would be here enjoying the moment except for the good fortune of our parents, or the luck of the draw to be born when and where we were, or to have encountered those few individuals who in every life make some key difference in the outcome. You and I, my friend, owe our good fortune to so many others whom we do not even know and who do not know us and whom for the most part we are never aware of at all. They in turn experience their own peculiar circumstances by a similar confluence of events, in what is an ever expanding network of connections. Yes, we are social creatures, my friend. The only question is on what scale. Even the hermit owes his solitude to those who tolerate him and make it possible for him to be left undisturbed.

That anyone could think what they have accomplished was due mostly to their own efforts shows a deplorable lack of imagination, or a delusional egomania. As you say, it is possible of course. Genius is another matter entirely. Yet not even genius is immune to indifference and can easily wither through neglect. I expect it is less the exception than we realize.

Though we disagree about most things, our long-suffering servant commands my deepest admiration. One can dismiss him by saying he simply does it for the money—I may have made that unkind accusation earlier—but I happen to know it is a lot more complicated than that. There is a great deal to admire. This evening, my friend, out of respect for him and all like him, why don't we stop kidding ourselves and get off to a fresh start? With this very first drink of the evening I propose a toast: To a new beginning. Let us drink to that before continuing.

You have listened patiently now for several evenings—indifferent but attentive, questioning and nodding politely. Surely by this time you must have seen through my little disguise. How long can one retreat from life? To see it always through the guise of some theory, hiding behind the protection of this mental construct, or that one, that explains nothing but merely obscures and conceals what one finds most threatening? It is life itself we are afraid of—not death. Resignation renders that threat impotent. Meanwhile we are in headlong flight, denying the one salvation available to us.

Such an attitude renders death the only truth, my friend, and death is no truth at all. It is merely a fact, and facts are never subject to judgment. Only by allowing the possibility of its denial can we assert whether death possesses any truth for us or not. It is a question to which I have nothing to add—others have dealt adequately with it. You know their conclusion: it is always possible to be convinced of whatever one is willing to believe. In that regard belief becomes little more than superstition, no matter what purpose lies behind it. I prefer to limit myself to those possibilities that precede death.

Through our paralyzing fear we are led to reject life. We seek to escape its inevitable demands and harsh realities, and thereby miss out also on its many joys and rewards. Yes, they are pleasures, in the original sense of that term—that which one finds pleasing. I should have called them that. Rewards suggests something we have a right to expect, and life carries no guarantees. Pleasure, however, is a term that lately has acquired a bad name. In the sternness of our present difficulties we have grown suspicious of any pleasure, preferring instead to hide behind our superstitions.

Hasn't pleasure led to the decay of society? Doesn't it produce unhappiness, pain, suffering, even death? These are stoical times. The burden of proof falls on the Epicurean. Call it indulgence or gratification or narcissism—whatever happens to be the buzzword of the moment. We see lurking behind it the secret desire for some forbidden pleasure, and we are on our guard. We are not yet free of that belief in the power of a few well chosen thou-shalt-not's to preserve society.

I am afraid we are by and large Protestants, my friend. Dark, gloomy souls who fear God and Satan equally. The God of the Old Testament—a harsh, demanding, vindictive God. The God of our fathers who wears the stern unrelenting countenance of an old man, for whom every pleasure of youth is but a bitter, forgotten memory. A God so bereft of pleasure cannot tolerate it in us.

I'm not talking here about what people do in church, what they profess. I'm talking about how they behave. Everywhere they are in retreat from life. They have denied its pleasures, forgotten its joys, renounced its happiness. They are afraid—to the point of continuing to breathe but ceasing to live. They cannot accept the only basis on which life must be lived.

I too tried for the longest time to deny those truths I saw staring at me in the mirror and to turn away. I was afraid to acknowledge them. To admit the truth of the face I saw was to admit that the time remaining to me was frighteningly short.

A mid-life crisis? Surely you cannot be serious. That term, like all of the other meaningless labels of our century, explains nothing. All of life, viewed that way, is a crisis. It is only a matter of when one first becomes aware. It can happen at any moment, on any street corner. Some of us are meant to live as aliens, discovering it later rather than sooner. It is a case of when one chooses to acknowledge and confront the inevitable. I am speaking of denial not realization. Even as I denied, I knew the truth of what I could not accept and had chosen to ignore at all costs. But life, my friend, cannot be denied. At some point I found that I could no longer continue the charade.

I moved into a small apartment by myself, down there among those lights, there where they are clustered the brightest. It was very plain and modest—I had discovered a need for simplicity. Let's be honest: it was practically shabby. The carpet was thin and worn. Through it you could feel every imperfection in the concrete floor underneath. The furniture was old and worn and soiled, stylish only by its abysmal lack of any redeeming grace or charm. The paintings on the wall were the most tasteless and garish pastels imaginable, mere decorations lacking any artistry—but I shall save speaking of them until later.

The walls themselves were concrete cinder block, painted but otherwise rough and unfinished. An inexpensive drape covered the small front windows. A sheer curtain hung across the only other window, above the kitchen sink, peering out the back. Except for a separate bath and vanity, the entire apartment consisted of one large room partitioned by a half cabinet separating the kitchen from the rest. A couch, a low table, one chair, two lamps, a small chest of drawers and a bare bookcase completed the furnishings.

Even so I lived better than most of the world's unfortunate people. I lacked nothing essential to my comfort and well being. I had running water, heat, and indoor plumbing. Yet when I moved into that apartment I became at once the alien I spoke of, a social deviant.

My behavior placed me outside the societal norm. I lived simply— well below my means—with no aspirations of improving my material surroundings. I had chosen an apartment in the less desirable section of town—the traditional abode in this country of those who are in transition, denied the status and respectability of home ownership and excluded from participation in the dream of private property. My comings and goings were private, even somewhat furtive. I knew none of my neighbors or had any real desire to. They, likewise, seemed preoccupied and intent upon their own affairs, isolated in a sort of self-absorption that they carried around with them like an invisible cocoon.

Yet I preferred it that way. I was bent on a measure of solitude.

I needed time to reflect, to be by myself, to listen if but briefly to that inexorable passage of time I had felt pulsing in my veins and seen staring back at me from the deepening lines etched on the face in the mirror. Any day during which I could not spend several hours alone, in a room by myself, left me apprehensive and fidgety.

I would sit and stare at my surroundings, and regard my situation. Doing so made the hours pass more slowly. I savored the experience of each breath, each quirky deviating thought that led me always down new paths in unexpected directions. I enjoyed the *deliberateness* of it. Afterwards, though I had done nothing, I felt as if I had accomplished some great work. The thoughts came in an unbroken sequence like the ticking of a clock in slow motion, and I could trace them back along a path strewn with the fitful starts and stops of a mental work of monumental proportions. I reached out with my thoughts and tugged at those hands, holding them back while I lived each moment to the fullest.

Yes, to the fullest, my friend. To do so does not require frenetic activity or the feverish pace we see all about us. That way too often obscures life. Life is truly lived in the resounding quiet of each moment. The other is merely its confirmation.

I began with just what was inside my tiny apartment until I knew every inch of it by heart, every detail no matter how insignificant. I sat in the deepening silence and drew my solitude about me like a cloak, and examined my surroundings.

At first I noticed mostly forms—the shape of the room, and then the shapes of its contents. The shape of the table was easy. That of the chair more difficult. For some of the shapes I had names, and those I could more easily categorize and dispense with. I would approximate and idealize. This shape was like a rectangular parallelepiped, that a cylindrical prism, another the frustum of a pyramid, and so on. Others, like the chair, I had to divide into parts in order to fit them into the categories for which I had names.

I made a game of devising ways ever more clever for dividing up the room and all of its contents into stacks and arrangements of regular shapes that, together, filled every available space. At first I concentrated on those objects and spaces where my scheme worked. The top of the table was reasonably like a plane, the base of the cabinet a rectangular parallelepiped. I soon found myself, however, drawn to those places where my scheme did not work—to the seams and edges and vertices in my imaginary stack of shapes. To a rounded corner, an irregular edge here, a chipped or uneven surface there. That was when I began to truly see my surroundings; by looking not at its regularities but at its exceptions. Not where it met my expectations, but where it confounded them. I noticed where the ceiling met the wall unevenly, where the Formica on the counter top was chipped and missing, how the cabinets bulged along one side, the grout that was gone from the tiles in the bathroom, the broken corner or edge of a cinder block in the wall. In short, my friend, I was seeing its flaws, its imperfections.

But as I continued to study them, they lost the character of flaws and took on the aspect of the place itself. Without them I would have been unable to see anything at all. The longer I looked the more I found that I could examine each one without ever exhausting its possibilities. No matter how many times I returned to even the simplest feature, I would discover something new, something else that had escaped my notice before. Each irregularity—I will no longer persist in calling them imperfections; they had ceased to be that—was an inexhaustible source of variety and detail. And the number of them kept multiplying. They had ceased to be irregularities even. They became instead the *reality* of what I saw. I realized again, my friend, that if there were even one irregularity, even a single deviation, then there would have to be an infinite number, until they and not their opposite constituted the real nature of the world.

In an instant my world was stood on its head. Transformed from an imagined orderly regularity to an infinite variety of endless deviation, with the result that for the first time I was finally able to see what I was looking at. Among other things it meant that no matter how often or how long I looked I could never see everything even in my simple one room apartment. Each time I would find something different from the way I had seen it or remembered it before. The power of memory was likewise diminished.

To find things always as we remember them, my friend; is it not a convenience and a comfort? Which of us has not substituted our memories for the real world and then clung desperately to them as the only refuge in an existence that defies understanding? A necessary illusion perhaps, but an illusion nonetheless, and one that diminishes the world and our experience of it. I took great comfort in the sudden expansion of my world, shrunk to this one room, to a complexity forever beyond my capacity to encompass it.

What's that? Surely some things remain the same; can always be counted on? Of course, my friend, but they are too simple and too few in number to matter. The sun rises and the sun sets. But after one realizes it, of what significance is it really? Like all the facts of our existence this one merely is. It is the endless variety of events between sunrise and sunset that most concerns us. What we can reduce to general principles becomes merely the backdrop against which all else takes place. But the very same principles allow a multitude—even an infinite number—of possible outcomes, all different in some respect. If we push it far enough we may even find that the general principles themselves are not absolute and inviolate.

In the beginning I noticed only the shapes of things, never the colors. The world I saw was made up of shadowy forms of light and dark. Not even black and white—that would have been too distinct—but various shades of gray in between. If I was aware of colors at all I could not recall them later but pictured whatever I had seen in simple tones of light and dark. The world that I held in my mind was like that seen in those gloomy canvases by the great landscape artists of the past—all full of light and shadows but devoid of any but the most morose and austere of colors.

Then I, like the Impressionist painters before me, discovered that shadows too have color. Nothing is ever black and white, or even shades of gray. All is color—in its infinite variation. It is we who make the world gray. If one looks closely the grays give way to color, and the color to other colors in finer and ever diminishing degrees of separation. We speak of a rainbow but that is nothing more than the general principle; sufficient to establish the *fact* of color, but too impoverished to do more than hint at the range of possibilities.

Which of the many colors that I now began to see in the once shadowy forms of my apartment can actually be found in the rainbow, my friend? None of them. They all occur in the many cracks and missing spaces of the general principle; in the seams and edges and at the vertices, as it were, where before my scheme of regular shapes could not portray the real world of forms that I saw. None of them is described by the general principle. Once more the same principle allows for a limitless number of possibilities—all different in some respect—until the real world, no matter how tiny and confined, is filled with unfathomable variety.

Even the purest colors of my world changed before my very eyes as I watched them, from the first light of dawn, to the shimmering brilliance of midday, to the translucence of dusk. The most subdued, like the pastel hues of my walls, defied every effort to render them static but were changed each time that I looked. Each shadow, every gradation of light, shifted the colors to different hues. It mattered where I sat, how long I stared. In a single shadow could be found an entire spectrum of color.

The physicists, my friend, have divided up our world into its component parts and their discrete characteristics, but to no avail. Matter has mass and charge and is composed first of molecules and atoms, then electrons and protons and neutrons, and now an increasing plethora of bits and pieces. Swarms of particles give way to ever more dense swarms with ever more foreign and mysterious properties. And still at the end one is left with the question any child can ask: but what is *that* made of? The description may be discrete, but only if one does not probe too far. Our world may have parts, but can any really believe it matters? What matters is the limitless variety that I observed in my tiny apartment.

As I sat in solitude and examined my surroundings I no longer noticed its shabbiness. Where before I had seen blemishes and flaws I now saw forms and colors, features and their endless details. I saw my world as it is, not as I might have imagined it to be. Not against some standard of regularity and order and perfection imposed upon it, by which to gauge its shabbiness or imperfection. That could come later. First I had to see it as it is.

Each time I looked it was as if I had created it anew and had never seen it before. And each time it wore a slightly different aspect. It was a work of endless satisfaction, never dull or boring but full of surprise and anticipation. I realized of course that I could never hope to know even the tiniest portion of my one room completely, and if not the tiniest portion then no portion at all and this world too would remain forever unknowable. That realization brought with it a satisfying reassurance.

Equally satisfying were the pleasant hours I spent studying its various details. Now the solitary work that before had seemed like one of monumental proportions was not limited to the helter skelter of my thoughts in haphazard directions, but embraced the complete marriage of mind and senses that uniquely defines us and places us squarely in the world. I delighted in the quiet hours of contemplation. My world took on an air of those stones and boulders strewn about the foothills around us. It was a world of the present—just as being in the presence of those silent stones grounds us so firmly in the here and now—yet a world that in its form and substance depended on the past and spoke directly of a future. There was about it an immediacy that linked it to both past and future.

I discovered in the pictures on my wall the same timeless quality—those paintings that I described to you earlier in such unflattering terms. I was giving you my initial reaction, before I learned to see them. When I finally opened my eyes those pictures underwent a remarkable transformation. Each was a scene from out of doors. A scene in the present, but so clearly in the present that it could have been any present and hence captured at once past, present and future in a single impression. In them time was frozen, made to stand still at some present moment, but a moment seen at an unspecified time in the past just as it might be again at some indeterminate time in the future, so that all of time was represented in each scene.

When I first inventoried my new surroundings I saw the pictures on the walls as single objects in the midst of other individual objects. Later, when my one room had expanded to become a world of inexhaustible detail, I realized that those pictures too were not single objects but were themselves the same source of infinite variety, that in each of them the painter had likewise depicted an entire world.

They were done in the *plein* air style of the Impressionists, full of bright, vivid colors true to life, without distinct boundaries or sharp forms, and with shadows composed of subtle gradations of color and form the way the eye actually sees the world. Not distinctly, but always a bit blurred when one tries to look too closely. For you see, my friend, the Impressionists in their paintings were attempting what we have been trying to do here. Far from painting indistinct smudges on his canvases Monet meant to show the world as it really looks, without sharp edges and with the separate colors placed on the canvas for the eye of the viewer to combine, the way one actually sees things.

The Impressionists found in their art a truer reality than the one they inherited from their predecessors, just as we are intent upon doing. Light was fundamental to their task, as it is to ours. They too found that light had a distinctive quality at each instant; one that constantly changed so that each scene had to be painted quickly to capture how it looked at that moment. Their world, like the one I had discovered in my room, was composed of an infinite variety of form and color, never static but always changing. Light in all its subtle nuances was essential to painting the reality they saw at each moment. They shunned the artificial light of the studio and painted instead out of doors, using natural light to reveal the truth of reality as they saw it. We too have been using a kind of natural light, my friend, to uncover the reality of life as it is. I am talking about the truth each of us comes to know in those unprotected moments when we lower our guard and set aside what we want to believe, what is easiest and most convenient and most comforting to believe, and instead confront what we know deep down we cannot deny.

No, of course I didn't think of those pictures in these terms. I had never even heard of the Impressionists. It is afterwards that one comes to organize an experience into ideas that can explain and interpret it, even then the ideas are never as important as the experience. We have made of the world an idea, when in truth it is an experience. What I experienced, my friend, was the realization that each of those pictures on my wall represented an entire world.

One in particular became my favorite. A landscape showing a grassy field dotted with too-large yellow and white flowers. Along one side a row of tall slender trees grew beside a stream. In the distance stood a green and brown farmhouse also oddly out of proportion to the remainder of the scene. Overhead stretched an endless pastel sky in which floated puffy, flat-bottomed clouds streaked with pink. The grasses in the field waved with the wind in perfect unison. The sun, nowhere visible, was everywhere apparent, and seemed to emanate from all directions. The people, also nowhere visible, were equally apparent. Nothing was indicated too precisely, everything was rather suggested, and the scene at a glance caught what the eye might at first view. There seemed not to be an overall perspective but rather three separate perspectives: that of the yellow and white flowers, which while scattered throughout the field were always in the foreground; that of the field and trees and sky, much as they might appear at a distance; and finally that of the farmhouse and the rest of the scene. Each of these three portions of the picture remained true to its own perspective, as though the artist had intentionally chosen to show the three parts separately.

I spent hours surveying that scene and studying it in detail. Nothing in it yielded any more precision to my careful eye than it had when first seen. No matter how long I looked or how closely I peered, the flowers, the trees and grasses, even the house retained the indistinct quality of objects at a distance. My mind had to supply what my eyes could not see, the way it did for objects out my window. The scene became not less, but more, real to me as a result. I could look at it forever without exhausting its possibilities.

In the blur of the grasses I could see the same fidelity that I saw in the green lawn outside my window. I could feel the wind blowing against my face and whispering in my ear. The colors were bright and complex, and the scene radiated sunlight from every surface, the way I remembered it from my childhood. The flowers seemed not to be growing in the ground at all but to be levitated above it, as if they stood for some separate and higher reality. The field and the sky stretched away to infinity, as though tunneling through the confining walls of my apartment to turn my one room inside out and open it onto the endless expanse of the outside world. The trees and the brook along one side kept the whole thing slightly off balance, the way reality so often is. The house in the center of the field reminded the viewer of the presence of people and connected the natural world to the man-made one. Everything was static, nothing changed, not the scene, not the light, yet I could feel the wind blow, see the grasses ripple and watch the flowers swaying in the breezes. The moment pictured there suggested all of time.

Each of the pictures on my wall was the same. A different view but each painted in the same fashion by the same hand true to the same principles, and each captured an entire world within its wooden borders. Anyone who had not learned to see things as I had would have found the cheap commercial quality of these reproductions, with their unfinished wooden frames, to be in perfect harmony with the shabby appearance and cheap decor of the rest of my apartment. In short, my friend, what had once been panels of the most garish and tasteless pastels imaginable had, upon more proper consideration, become the perfect art for this place and time. With it my little world had been further expanded and enriched, and the inside of my one room joined onto all that lay outside of it.

But how do I know any of that was what the artist intended? Maybe there was no intent at all. Maybe there was not even an artist, only a craftsman. Maybe the only intent was to paint a wall decoration to sell and make money. What of it? The artist alone does not get to make art, my friend. The artist must have his audience. Only together can they make art.

How many artists have been surprised by what their admirers saw in their work and made of it? How many have not realized themselves exactly what they were up to, until an admiring public convinced them of it? How many others have complained bitterly that their work was misunderstood, or praised for the wrong reasons? And how many have put aside their principles—and their qualms—and blindly accepted the adulation of the crowd in order to be able to go on doing what they wanted to anyway? Those who have not would be the exception, my friend, and we include in their number even the greatest.

Was it I, or the painter who did not even bother to sign them, that made the pictures on my wall into art, the perfect art for this place and time? Who was the real artist here? The one who painted them? Or the one who found in them some meaning that the painter may never have foreseen or intended? Who actually created the world that I saw painted in those pictures on my wall, and gave them the quality that made them art? Where do we draw the line between life and art anyway?

It is best not to try to answer, my friend. We are all artists in the final analysis. To those who are truly aware, there can be no separation between life and art.

7

Ah, there you are. Here before me, I see. Is it possible, my friend, you're anxious to continue? Well, I apologize for yesterday's rather abrupt ending. Let me begin by first answering the question you asked before we parted: No, my friend, I did not go on to become an artist, the same way I had once embraced becoming the consummate scientist-technician. I was talking about a certain frame of mind—the adoption of an attitude, or rather an outlook on life—when I made that remark last evening. My story is not suddenly going to become that of Van Gogh or Gauguin, who in mid-life turned from other—and, I might add, most unlikely—callings to become painters and professional artists. But, like them, the change that came over me was no less profound or determining. I was seized by the same intensity and passion, only without the madness. As the sanguine Renoir remarked when he met Van Gogh, "Sir, you paint like a madman."

They told Van Gogh he couldn't draw, and you no doubt have witnessed for yourself Gauguin's modest attempts. But their evaluations were as irrelevant as those that do not distinguish science from technology. They were mistaking technique and the mere technician for art and the real artist. The former is but a craft and can be handled as well by a hack as by a genius. The latter is a new way of looking at the world—indeed, a way of creating the world anew each moment—in which the component of genius is unmistakable and that, as I said, recognizes no demarcation between art and life. Life is the continual unfolding of art; art is the constant expression of life.

Within the confines of my little world I slowly began to erase that dividing line without even being aware of it. Just as I had learned to see the true nature of my modest surroundings, I now spent long hours admiring and contemplating those pictures on my wall, until the distinction between them and the rest of my surroundings had vanished altogether. I came to view the creation of such works of art as a worthwhile and enviable accomplishment. I felt the stirring of an urge to create some work of my own, though I had not the vaguest notion of what that meant, or how I might go about it.

The interpretation of those paintings that I had come to in my long hours of contemplation became itself an undertaking of immense satisfaction, and partially fulfilled the creative urge I felt. I thought through my ideas carefully, until I was convinced that I had addressed every angle and thought of every issue, that I had anticipated every possible question and had worked out an appropriate response. At length I had constructed a thorough analysis of each of the paintings individually, one that also encompassed them collectively. I had fashioned, my friend, a theory of art, or at least the art those paintings represented to me.

I will tell you in all honesty, I was quite pleased with myself. I even went so far as to make notes, and then put the whole thing into writing, trying to detail each salient point and to construct an argument that would be as ironclad and convincing as I could possibly make it. I worked feverishly at it. Each time I thought I was finished I would think of another weakness in my analysis, and revise the whole thing again. I would awake in the middle of the night with some new point to include, get out of bed and work until dawn, trying to patch whatever difficulties my new idea had uncovered.

I learned how frustratingly difficult it is to say anything for which there is not some conceivable exception or counterexample. I worked always to find those plain unadorned sentences that would state the simple, incontestable truth. As I wrote each one I would strike out all that was not absolutely essential, anything for which I could see some potential contradiction, any assertion in which I could imagine some shortcoming, until I had literally crossed out everything I meant to say.

In the process I discovered again how difficult it is, my friend, to convey by reason what the heart knows to be true. Not everything can be supported by reason. What can be explained is not poetry, said Yeats. Some things one must simply accept in order to get any further. There is the truth of the physicist, and that of the poet, just as there are the separate truths of the head and the heart. Of what value is the one in trying to understand the other?

As I labored to reduce my argument to those unadorned declarative sentences that stated the plain truth, I could find no inviolate general principles—except those I was willing to accept without question. Yet I remained convinced of my analysis and committed to my theory, for I had arrived at it not by reason and logic but by some process more difficult to describe, based on my experience of the pictures on my wall. The reason and logic had been added later, to make what I already knew to be true sound more convincing. What was missing from those simple declarative sentences was that spark of passion I felt about those paintings: the passion that represented the distilled essence of my experience of them. I found it especially difficult trying to put that passion into words; much more difficult than trying to construct a reasoned argument. And here was yet a new danger. That I might convince someone else, or be convinced myself—by passionate persuasion—of something not worth believing. For when we abandon reason we do so at our own peril.

I did the best I could. I based my argument on a few general principles grounded in the passion derived from my experience of the paintings. The rest followed more or less logically from that. Finally I was satisfied. I wrote the whole thing up, revised a few minor points, and felt pleased with the result.

At the completion of my little project I experienced a strange emptiness, and a longing I had not known before. At first I passed it off to the boredom that sets in following the completion of any intense mental activity. I told myself that I had not been getting enough exercise, that I had been too long absorbed in my thoughts. I broke my solitude and took long walks. When that didn't satisfy me I took up running, gradually extending the time devoted to it until I was running several miles each day. I found the intense aerobic activity, and the release of chemical endorphins that it stimulated, extremely pleasurable. I experienced the runner's high—the feeling of euphoria caused by the body's natural response to the extreme stress of aerobic exercise.

I was transformed. I began to crave the excruciating pleasure produced by the pain of physical exertion. At such moments I thought great thoughts, became capable of great works, shed all my inhibitions and dared to think of myself in new and transforming ways. Under the influence of my new chemical ego I became assertive, bold—even daring—and self-confident. No one and nothing intimidated me, or could deter me from thinking myself capable of any task. The most difficult questions yielded to fresh approaches that I had never before imagined—and mostly couldn't recall afterwards. I could decide any issue without the least indecision or hesitation. I had no reluctance to assert my will, to think in terms of *my* wishes, *my* needs, *my* best interest. And I did so without regret or remorse or feelings of guilt. Suddenly everything seemed simple and straightforward. I felt truly liberated.

I took my problems and went running, my friend. I looked forward eagerly to those daily sessions. Soon I began to crave them and had organized my entire life around them. I became an addict in every sense of the term.

Whenever I was not under the influence of those marvelous chemical liberators I became mired in inaction, unable to do anything, to make even the simplest decisions. I would put off deciding anything or taking any action until I could leave everything else behind and go running. Even that did not always work and I began to run farther, push myself harder, until I was near the point of physical exhaustion. Many of the things I did under the influence of that new-found euphoria later seemed ill-advised or made no sense to me at all. I was at the mercy of my addiction. And like the addict, the solitude of my thoughts was replaced by the solitude of my addiction. I had traded my mental solitude for an equally isolating physical one. I took my problems and went running, but in actuality I outran few of them. The deepest ones were always there at the finish to greet me when I came down from my temporary high.

No matter the form of solitude, my friend, it is still solitude. The real cause of that strange emptiness I felt was just my seclusion and isolation. My longing was one of loneliness. When I put my thoughts about art in writing it was because of an unrealized need to share them with someone else. I could not keep bottled up inside me the intense feelings I had uncovered. The understanding I had come to about those paintings was too remarkable and too important to be kept secret. My own excitement about it was impossible for me to contain. I had to tell someone about my remarkable discovery.

Writing—the kind of writing I was doing, my friend—is an admission of the need to share the thoughts and feelings that drove my pen feverishly across the page. To share them with another person, with someone capable of understanding and verifying our own experience; someone capable of validating the passion that leads us to struggle to find our thoughts, and then to further struggle to find words capable of expressing those thoughts, and then to continue the struggle until we have captured and synthesized the unique union of language and feeling that expresses what one recognizes as the simple truth, without need of any further proof. We may say it is only for ourselves, but if so, why bother? Why would anyone engage in such a monumental struggle hour upon hour, day after day, years on end in many cases, only to say again what one already knows and believes—if not driven by some unspoken need to share those thoughts and feelings with another human being? Think of it the next time you hear someone who has invested a life's work in this struggle denounced as a misanthrope, or condemned for holding up to us an unfavorable view of ourselves, or taken to task for exposing the darker side of our nature. You know the saying, "No greater love hath any man..."

I had made something, and having made it I found that was not enough. I also needed to share it with someone. Don't misunderstand me; I clung to my solitude, and any day during which I could not spend time alone still left me nervous and apprehensive. But my solitude also made me crave the company of others, just as the crush of the crowds made my time alone more vital and precious.

"I existed in the midst of throngs, yet I was increasingly lonely." How often we hear it said, my friend. There is no contradiction in it, I assure you. There is nothing more isolating than *plenitude*. By it we are separated from ourselves, which is the most suffocating kind of isolation. We are forced to adopt whatever guise is necessary to deal with the mass of humanity about us; indeed, to take on whatever guise may be *imposed* by that mass of humanity as a condition of our survival. First one identity may be appropriate. Then in a different situation another is necessary. Then another and another, until we have become so many different actors playing so many roles that one character playing one part at this moment is largely oblivious to another character acting some other part at another moment. And we, unaware of them all, are aware only of our growing sense of alienation and the increasing loneliness we feel. Desperate to retain some individual identity to which we can remain true we retreat into that inner self we recognize as our one true being, while putting on whatever disguises are required to get us through the day. Finally the schism between the inner self and that outward cast of actors widens to the point where we are cut off and trapped, unable to escape and reconnect the inner self to the outside world. We become that modern phenomenon: the schizophrenic being.

I did not wish to surrender the independence and identity that in my solitude I had gained. Yet the impulse that led me to write out my thoughts so carefully, that left me with that strange emptiness and longing afterwards, also led me to seek the company of others. No matter that I did not understand why, or think about it in quite these terms. At the very least I felt a kind of ennui so typical of our schizophrenia.

Yet where, my friend, does one go to seek company these days? Not to the theater; not to concerts or museums or places of entertainment; not even to church anymore. Yes, this establishment would be superior to any of those. Those places are outmoded artifacts of a time gone by. The cultural identity they signify was one seldom realized in practice anyway. They stand for past experiments that have all failed, or that were never truly representative. Sports? No, those too are mostly entertainment and represent but a small segment of who we really are.

To find company of the kind I mean one must go to the true cultural center of the society. Yes, my friend: to the shopping mall.

We are a culture defined by our materialism. By our possession of material things that we buy in search of an identity, then discard to buy again in an attempt to find some other identity. What binds us together— the only thing we share in common anymore—is our possession of material objects, which we possess merely because everyone else does, and because they are the only means we have found that satisfies our need to share something in common. Until ironically we have not acquired the individual identity we set out to find through the possessions we own, but one collective identity based on the ownership of possessions.

It is perhaps the most honest expression of culture possible. We have been pointed in this direction for a long time—for most of our history. All of the other great synthesizing ideas—knowledge, science, art, music, literature, government, religion—have only served to divide us into more and more factions, and have one by one succumbed to this other great organizing principle or else have been enlisted in its service. Those cultures not organized around the acquisition of material goods have given way to those that are—as will all eventually.

The shopping mall is the true symbol of our culture. It replaces the medieval marketplace where everyone met to barter and swap and trade, to gossip and discuss private affairs, to make deals, to flirt, court, arrange marriages and conduct all social intercourse. Now we go to the mall. Increasingly our affairs are conducted there, and eventually all will be. Every town has its shopping mall. The only ones that do not are those smaller than the typical mall. Cities are defined in terms of those having more than one mall, which then serve to identify the various districts. Stature among cities is measured by the number and size of shopping malls, and all vie to maintain a reputation for the grandest and most opulent. When I ventured out of my apartment in search of company, my friend, it was quite natural that I would seek it at the mall.

I went there in the evenings or on weekends when the obligations of work could be set aside and people had time for more important pursuits. Then they would flock to the mall, and I would immerse myself in the crowds. I must admit I was fascinated by the dazzling array of things to be found in all those neat, glass-fronted shops. A more impressive display of the ingenuity and inventiveness of the human mind is hard to imagine. I would wander in and out for hours on end, just trying to see all of the different items. I would find things whose use I could not conceive until it was explained to me. There were others that even with my training I could not fathom the inner workings of, and could only guess at how they operated. I played a game in which I would imagine that I needed an item for such and such a purpose, then go off in search of it. Rarely if ever did I dream up any want or need for which I could not find some article that would serve the purpose. There were equally many superfluous and unnecessary items; it was in the creation of these that the human capacity for invention was perhaps the most impressive. Knickknacks, trinkets, crafts, objets d'art—the array was endless, changed constantly, and never exhausted the seemingly limitless possibilities.

There were stores like enormous warehouses, filled with hardware, tools, building supplies, home and garden needs. There one could find everything required to build and furnish a house, cultivate a garden, landscape and care for a lawn—or construct an entire community or city. There were clothing stores, groceries, bakeries. I could imagine a vast network of factories and workshops filled with people producing all these goods, linked to the shopping malls by a far-flung network of highways and railroads and supply lines with the means to transport those goods from the factories to the stores, where those same people and others like them would come to see and admire and acquire them, in an unending and ever repeated sequence that correctly depicts the real workings of this society. It is this more than any characteristic of government or religion or background or language that unites us and describes who we are.

The shopping mall is the hub, the central institution. From it all the tentacles of society radiate outward, and to it all paths lead in turn. It is the shopping mall that symbolizes the central motivating fantasy of our society: that out there somewhere is an inexhaustible assortment of wonderful things that are ours to acquire. This fantasy—and not all the meaningless theories about capital and greed and exploitation—is what explains capitalism. Governments have been toppled, or more recently merely discarded, for failure to live up to it, and they will be again. It is this fantasy and not the empty rhetoric about duty, responsibility, family and belief in God that binds us together. Materialism has not caused the collapse of society, my friend; it is what sustains us and keeps it going.

In the central plazas and along the covered walkways of the mall were art exhibits, antique shows, displays of local crafts, automobile and boat shows, even carousels and carnival rides for the youngsters. In my leisure I would wander, browse, examine or just sit on the stone benches and watch the crowds. I did not often shop or purchase anything—although on occasion I felt compelled to buy something as a gesture of politeness, or as a way of paying some small fee for admission to this magnificent spectacle. All about me were bustling adults, efficient and business-like, who wasted little time or effort; frolicsome and exuberant children; clannish and awkward youths; self-absorbed young lovers; old people; whole families together. Those of means and others of no means. Those who were there mainly to be seen, and those trying to escape notice. And those like myself merely there to be there because this was where everyone else was.

There were of course sounds and noises, even music, the bustle and hum of all human enterprise. But the sounds soon faded into a smooth homogeneous background, against which I was no longer aware of any variations, and which I did not hear so much as I felt it closing in around me like a protective mantle. I found the steady indistinct roar, like the enveloping silence of my room, soothing and conducive to concentrating on my thoughts. I watched, fascinated by the amusement of the crowds.

At first I could see little, just as when I first began to observe my surroundings sitting alone in my one room apartment. I could of course see the complexity and multitude of forms and colors; I had learned to be expert at that. It was the people themselves I had not yet learned to see. I watched them move, act, interact, behave—yet I did not understand how to really see what I was observing. Here was a world whose complexity went far beyond that of substance and mere form and color, beyond any of the physical senses, to encompass the same mysterious consciousness that I had felt in the beating heart of the universe pulsing beneath my fingertips. I thought again of that detached observer of the human condition I had imagined in my youthful innocence—removed and peering down on the human panorama, observing and cataloging it as something of a natural historian, in an attempt to describe it and in that description to finally understand it. As I observed even the simplest most straightforward actions, I realized the unbreachable gulf that separates such a scientific impulse from the true complexity of the real world, a world whose unfolding intricacy leads us down paths stretching always beyond our understanding.

I noticed first the actions of happy, joyful, carefree people. Their behavior seemed the most transparent and the least difficult for me to understand. About everything they did there was a genuine openness and honesty, unmistakable and easy to read. They seemed to want or need little beyond what they had, and appeared content to defer to others. They were, in a word, ingenuous, my friend; and if matters had stood there my task would have been easy enough. The difficulty lay in all the many reasons there are for being disingenuous—and in all the many ways. I observed jealousy, rivalry, anger, fear, shame, rejection; malice, hatred, anguish and despair; each of them in varying degrees and all clearly evident in the faces and actions of those milling crowds that passed nightly through the shops and corridors of that vast human arena.

As I wandered about or merely sat and watched, I became acutely aware of how little I knew about human behavior. I do not mean understanding, my friend, but the most rudimentary experience and knowledge out of which to fashion some deeper understanding. I had set all such questions aside long ago as unanswerable, and hence unimportant. Now I realized that for that very reason—because they are unanswerable, even unfathomable—they were the most important questions of all. For they and all the impenetrable mysteries make our world what it is.

I found it impossible to get out of my mind the sadness and the desperation that I saw stamped on those faces I encountered in my nightly excursions. The carefree laughter and simple joy never quite offset the wrenching looks or the bowed heads and stooped shoulders of those whose cares seemed to weigh so heavily upon them. I felt overwhelmed by the need to reach out to them. Suddenly my poor thoughts about art and the pictures on my wall seemed trivial and pointless. Imprinted on those faces and on those burdened features were questions in the presence of which I felt helpless and inadequate. What answer can one offer when one is not even aware of the question, my friend? I wanted to speak, but I had nothing to say.

I had intended to observe; to learn to understand their behavior the way I had those paintings on my wall. But this would require more than simply learning a new way to see or a different way of thinking about what I observed. Alas, this would require a life's work grounded in the sum of all the individual experiences of those I observed, all that they had encountered to cause them the joy and the pain, the happiness and the sorrow that I saw mirrored in their features. Nothing less would ever be adequate to comprehend it. No theories of psychology, no Pavlovian or Skinnerian attempts to reduce the complexity of their actions to some scheme of cause and effect. No invention of categories or compartments into which we can neatly stuff the components of our behavior to keep them separate and thus simplify them to the point where they become meaningless. No psychoanalytical mumbo-jumbo or voodoo-ism by which one can explain everything by never explaining anything. No, my friend; to understand what I saw looking back at me from all those happy, carefree, sorrowful, anguished faces, I would have to come to know, to live, to experience what they had experienced. To fathom *how* they behaved I would have to understand *why* they behaved.

I would have to live all those lives myself. To cram all of that living into one life—think of it. Even if it were possible I am not sure anyone would desire it. You know the saying: "You only live once, but if you do it right, once is enough." There is much in our experience that makes the allotted span of three score and ten seem about right. To be forever young—would it not be the greatest curse imaginable? Or to suffer indefinitely the indignities and trials of old age? Or to be always in transition between the two? To have the normal pace of change that we find in the seasons of our lives slowed and arrested to a creeping boredom? To those who would wish it one is tempted to say, "Give them in earnest what they ask for in jest."

I had only one life to live, my friend, and not that much of it. Alone, I could not hope to understand the complexity of human behavior in such a short span. I would have to enlist the collected findings of all those tormented souls who had tried before me. I am speaking of those imaginative works of literature, and of all the poets who created them. What I had dismissed before as meaningless now seemed to hold the only hope of finding the meaning I sought.

I did not know where to start. I wandered into one of the bookstores in the mall. I made my way past the myriad works whose covers promised—all for the meager price of a book—to give answers to all of our questions about how-to, how-not-to, when-to, where-to, why-to and what-to. I came finally to that diminishing section where are shelved a dwindling portion of the enduring works that we in our collective judgment have decided represent the relevant stories of our experiences, those that promise merely to show us questions for which there are *no* answers. I hesitantly chose a volume from the shelf and leafed through its pages, reading sporadically here and there before deciding I would purchase it. Though I had never read it, I knew of it. Hurriedly I chose several others I had also heard of, and retreated.

During the subsequent evenings I sat in my room and read. I read for a long time, my friend. One might almost say of me that in my middle years I surrounded myself with solitude and read. Novels, plays, poetry, memoirs, personal reflections, essays, fiction, non-fiction—the form mattered not at all, the content was everything. I read haphazardly, though avidly. I sampled everything I came to but read only those that spoke to me. When I discovered one whose words seemed aimed directly at me, I read everything by the same author I could get my hands on until I had exhausted all that each writer had to say to me. For most it was not hard to do. Most had only one book in them and kept saying the same things over and over again. Some could find new and imaginative ways of repeating themselves, or language that was beautiful and captivating, and to these I would return for a little while. But finally I got the message and moved on to seek what else I could discover. Some did not speak to me at all. Those I made a special effort to engage, trying again or with some other work, but usually without success. Some vital link was missing, some common experience or necessary spark of interest we did not share. After that I would abandon them so they would not stand between me and those others whose words instantly touched something basic at the core of my being.

One or two wormed their way so completely into my mind I felt they knew my every thought, all my darkest secrets, my most terrible fears, and were pointing their accusing fingers at my tormented and guilty soul. On those occasions I would feel such relief and joy as I had never known. I was not alone after all. There were others who had experienced the same fears, the same angst-ridden emotions, and who could confront them, put them into language so compelling and honest that it would seize me by the throat and leave me sweating, my pulse racing, my chest tightened as though clamped in a vise, struggling to catch my breath. I would be drained by the experience, exhausted and limp, yet with such a sweet taste of victory and such boundless unspeakable joy that I wished to immerse myself that much deeper into what had drained and exhausted my emotions. To such writers I returned until I had read everything they had to say. I envied them their courage and honesty, their skill, the understanding I was sure they must possess in order to put into words those truths that, alone, I had been unable to face. Surely here was the understanding I was searching for.

No, I was not reading for entertainment, my friend, though I confess I was entertained by my reading. I quickly exhausted the possibilities of comedy. It was all too easy to laugh, and it did not seem necessary to question the reasons why. My sense of humor? But of course, can't you tell? I do have a sense of humor—livelier now than ever. But in these times it seems only polite, my friend, to first earn the right to indulge in open laughter.

I focused instead on those troubling works that others find most unentertaining. In them I searched for answers to my questions. Some merely pretended answers, and to those I gave a knowing smile and moved on. Those whose answers were the most troubling most held my attention. The more disturbing the answer, the more lengthy and careful my consideration of it. Only the most unsettling explanations satisfied my appetite for the truth. Those that were too simple or reassuring I knew to be false. As someone has said, "Well a question ain't really a question if you know the answer, too." A question that has no answer is already disturbing enough, too disturbing to accept a soothing reassurance. Such questions demand equally disquieting responses if they are to be believable.

I was profoundly affected by all those troubling works I read. I could not get enough of them. The more I read the more deeply touched I was, and the more I yearned to read. In a polymathic frenzy I resolved to read them all, every single work I could lay my hands on. I read with unabated frenzy each waking moment of the day, and far into the wee hours of every night. I was convinced that hidden in the pages of some book I had not read I would eventually find the meaning of life I was looking for. Surely the wisdom that had produced such courageous and revealing insights into the disturbing nature of the world had somewhere, in one of those books, put its finger on the secret we are all searching for, in possession of which we would finally have the truth of life as it should be. I neglected my work, my friends, even myself. None but the most essential duties could tear me from my reading.

Yes, I read that book too—several times in fact. I confess that I had never done so before, though I had read small portions, and others had told me what was in it all my life. I was surprised—I might even say shocked—to discover what was not in it, when I finally read it for myself. Except for its endless chronicle of failure, in which I found a certain unthwartable magnificence, there was little else of interest to me. In the first portion, frankly, the story grows tiresome by repetition—though I confess to a grudging admiration for such unflagging persistence in the face of constant failure and the vengeance of a wrathful God. I kept thinking to myself, 'When are these people going to get it?', but then that was just the point, wasn't it? The second portion is only a clever ruse to keep one from asking the very questions that drove me in my search. It did not even offer hope, but merely substituted for hope an unconvincing and unsustainable lie in an attempt to persuade us to abandon the search. Only Job, and the author of Ecclesiastes, were admirable. Even there one had to stop before reaching the end. The ending in each case is just cheating by someone later who couldn't face the awful truth. As I said before, it is always possible to be convinced of what one is willing to believe. I preferred to doubt all but the most obstinate and obdurate truths.

I was not at all put off or discouraged by those disturbing works I read. Quite the contrary. I was reassured by what I found there. It was reaffirming to know that my experience of the world was not an aberration; that my world was not unlike the ones created by those fertile imaginations out of their own experiences, for we at least had that much in common. I felt close to all the frightened, lonely, desperate people I had seen in my life. I felt as though we shared something, something that was at the heart of what it means to be human. I wanted even more to reach out to them. The way I had wanted to when I put my thoughts about the paintings on my wall into writing, then felt a sense of longing to show them to someone else. This time however I did not experience the same kind of loneliness. Now I did not feel alone at all, though I may have been. This time I felt the kinship of being united in our common condition, all of us together.

I continued my frenetic search almost to the point of collapse. The piles of books stacked on my table and the floor of my apartment grew until they covered every available space and tottered precariously, threatening to collapse in a heap along with the aspirations that led me to seek truth in those mountains of pages. As I finished each one I would lay it hurriedly aside to begin another. Some I kept coming back to, to read again and again. I took to highlighting the passages that struck me as significant, until the pages of my most treasured volumes fairly glowed with the fluorescence of my underlining. Always I searched out those passages where I might discover the answer I was seeking. Or out of which I might piece it together by combining the underlined sections, like mathematical equations, in some way that my reading would reveal to me. Bleary eyed I stuck doggedly to my goal of finding the meaning of life in those worn pages, the understanding of life as it should be, my friend. Until, finally, I did collapse—the total collapse of utter futility.

I was forced to admit what I had realized from the beginning, what by now had been driven home too many times. Alas, the meaning of life is not to be found in the pages of a book, my friend. Not any book. Those writers I so admired who moved me so deeply were no different in what they did from the scientists before them. Like the artist who painted the pictures on my wall each one had created a tidy little world of his own, captured in those beguiling words marching endlessly through the pages of the volumes strewn about my floor. But these too were artificial worlds, populated with made-up people who were merely puppets dangling at the ends of strings. They and everything that happened to them unfolded in perfect obedience to the will of their creators, the way the tidy determinants of classical physics obeyed the workings of immutable natural law. Each of these worlds, like those in the paintings on my wall, was intended by the artist to describe some truth of the real world. But they were not the real world, merely imperfect descriptions. They were like those mysterious symbols I had drawn upon my wall, by which the reassuring world of determinism could be set down and understood.

And like the descriptions of the scientist, these stories too were limited. The real world defies description. Like the atoms of the physicist it is neither wave nor particle but both at the same time, a reality that can only be depicted in metaphor, fuzzy always at the edges and blurred whenever we try to look too closely. That is why the best stories tell only by showing us. The most difficult things cannot be said. They must be dramatized and acted out, as they are in life, for each to draw his own conclusions and find his own meaning. What cannot be seen clearly, like the images in an Impressionist painting, can only be hinted at and suggested, the way the mind as well as the eye actually perceives the world. Yes, I assure you, we have been doing that same thing here in our story.

The world of the artist, like that of classical physics, is deterministic. But the real world does not unfold in perfect obedience to the will of the artist. Art is *like* life, my friend, but it is *not* life. I would have to look elsewhere for the understanding that I sought.

No, I do not still live in that apartment. I gave it up long ago for much different surroundings. Like Thoreau I never had any intention of abandoning the world. Back then I only wanted to find some way of living in it on my own terms. Now, at last, I am content with far less.

8

My friend, over here! Hello again. Yes, I have been here for some time already. I purposely arrived earlier than usual this evening. For some reason I felt a sudden urge to come early and indulge my interest in observing the antics of my customers. With your permission, my friend, let us spend this evening relaxing and enjoying our leisure on the terrace, from where we can look out upon that brilliant flowering of humanity spreading across the desert. Recounting last evening my impulse to immerse myself in throngs reminded me of just how much I should regret their not being there. Regret exactly what, my friend? Why the entire spectacle of this divine—and, yes, heroic—comedy, and even my own insignificant part in it.

Whatever else we may ponder in the quiet of our solitude, we all yearn to find some way of understanding life. And everyone who has felt that yearning, along with all the poets and artists who have struggled to depict it for themselves and, in so doing, for us, are comrades alike in a common enterprise. It is not just the most brilliant or gifted whose responses to the world count, but those of the most ordinary and commonplace among us, those who frequent this establishment and the keepers of all those individual lights, my friend.

Come. Our table and our drinks await us. Shamelessly, I have exercised that privilege of which I spoke the other evening to secure for us the best accommodations of the house. Never mind. It is a harmless indulgence. No one will begrudge it of us. After all, there should be some small reward for your patience and perseverance the last few evenings. These others realize your ordeal. You are kind to say so, my friend, but believe me I understand how much I am in your debt.

But no, my friend. I most certainly did not give up the search. Even now it continues. I still pour through those troubling works of our time hoping to come across the true meaning of life. I realize it is futile. I think that I must always have known it. But it is the quest that matters, not just the outcome. Just because some goal is without possibility is no reason to abandon the effort. That is just the point at which to begin in earnest, my friend. If the goal is worthwhile, its futility merely renders the attempt heroic.

You must have had to drive through that throng of angry demonstrators as you arrived this evening. Yes, they had us surrounded, didn't they? Some days in this city every approach is cut off by one group or another, protesting or supporting something. If it isn't smoking it is alcohol or marijuana or carbon dioxide or polluted air or war or whatever. Exactly *what* does not matter. There are so many causes it becomes impossible to keep up with them all. Once they picketed this establishment when I refused to ban smoking from the premises. In acknowledgment we bought a round for the house and drank to their health. Afterwards we all lit up. I would have invited them in for drinks, but nowadays everyone is so grim and humorless I did not dare risk it. Yes, I would agree. Upon occasion their demonstrations can be trying, and a great inconvenience to commerce and peace of mind.

A nuisance? Perhaps. But if so, it is a nuisance well worth tolerating, my friend. Once or twice I have been in their ranks and I may be again at the right moment. They are the legions of followers who have dedicated themselves to some great cause despite the odds against them. Most have little or no chance of succeeding. The desperate plight of whatever cause they espouse usually testifies to that. Most often they are a small minority, yet they can be quite vocal—and influential. It is the nobleness of their cause—together with the futility of their mission—that gives them their special status. In their own way they are reaching out to us; by their actions reminding us. They awake in us dormant memories of our need to rebel now and then. Thank God we cannot be talked out of it.

In my reading I had discovered that natural expression of one's innermost thoughts and feelings. I mean lyrical poetry, my friend. And my need to reach out to others took the form of first reaching out to myself in simple verses. One Sunday as I sat at my table reading I was seized by a sudden urge to say something to all those tortured souls whose torment I had so joyously experienced in my reading; a torment that deliciously mirrored my own, real or imagined. I did not know what to say. As I sat there mute, struggling for some expression of my urge to acknowledge the common bond uniting us, I picked up my pencil and without hesitation hurriedly wrote out the verses to a simple poem. It was all about intending to write a poem, out of words that never came, and the thoughts that I was thinking just fell like April rain, to be soaked up by the garden of memories in my mind, where they nurture other thoughts that I will use another time...something to that effect, my friend.

Out of this abortive first attempt I had at least managed to say something that confirmed the sincerity of my intentions, even if the result was destined only for my eyes. From time to time other such spontaneous outpourings caught me by surprise. Very few of them were the result of any conscious effort. Rather they just happened, like a cry of joy or a sudden sob that comes from nowhere. I took to writing them down the instant they occurred to me. Those I didn't were lost forever, much to my regret. The pure joy those simple utterances brought me was excruciating, and only heightened my need to tell someone what I was experiencing. Soon I had a pile of scrap paper on which I had jotted down in crude verses whatever thoughts popped into my mind. Each time, I felt as though an enormous burden had been lifted, that I had been joined in conversation with the world even if it were a one-sided exchange. You must remember that other stanza by the Belle of Amherst: "This is my letter to the world, That never wrote to me,—The simple news that nature told, With tender majesty..." I mention them at all merely to convince you of the depth of my need to express what I had kept bottled up inside for too long.

I had grown desperate for companionship, for some form of contact that went beyond the superficial. For true intimacy, my friend. I tried creating it for myself in poetry, then later in stories like those I had been reading. But that attempt only reinforced my need to experience the real world, and real intimacy, not one of my own creation. Alas, how else can I put it? I began a series of abortive affairs.

One afternoon as I was returning to my apartment the woman who lived next to me was standing in her open doorway. She often sat in a chair just outside her door in the warm sunshine and watched me come and go, but previously she had never spoken or even acknowledged my presence. To tell the truth I had the feeling she regarded me with a measure of disdain and a deep suspicion. She was very dark and had serious, almost somber features. I found her attractive but in her presence I could not help feeling uncomfortable, even somewhat disturbed. Possibly because I had lain awake at night listening as she and her husband made love with just the thin bare wall between us. Certainly on none of the other occasions when she sat and watched me go by had our eyes ever met the way they did that day. There was about her stare a look of such yearning and intensity that I was arrested in my motion. Those dark eyes were like bottomless pools drawing me in. I could feel myself being pulled toward her even as she took one step backwards into her apartment. Neither of us said anything; and now an awkward silence grew up. I felt compelled to speak and nervously stammered out something that only deepened my discomfort. Finally I managed to collect my wits and invited her to come inside with me for a cup of coffee.

It was a totally inappropriate and meaningless gesture, but that seemed not to matter to either of us. As I pushed the door to my apartment closed and heard the crisp metallic click of its latch, I turned and found her eyes still searching mine, still tugging at me the way they had when they brought me up short outside her door. I don't know what possessed me next, but I reached out and took her in my arms and kissed her. Foolishly, I blurted out that I had listened through the wall to her making love. That confession unleashed such a flood of pent-up emotion that we exhausted ourselves in love-making, until at last we fell asleep in each other's arms. Perhaps I should have said we exhausted ourselves in satiating our lust, but at that moment no one could have distinguished between the two. Those who claim to see a distinction are simply afraid of their emotions, or their motives, or else reveal their own inhibitions. Later that afternoon when I awoke she was gone. The next day her apartment was empty. She and her husband had left. I lay awake at night listening to the sounds of silence coming through the wall. I never saw her again.

During the days and nights following I could not get her out of my mind. Nor could I even realize what had happened—or imagine why. It seemed as if it had never occurred; that I could still see her sitting outside her doorway, hear her making love through the wall at night. But then I would remember how she had looked at me with those dark, bottomless eyes, the deep sleep from which I awoke to find her gone, and I would wonder again, why?

A few weeks later some revelers on their way to a party knocked at my door by mistake, and then to cover up their embarrassment invited me to join them. I accepted, and we ended up at the apartment of a young lady who even at that age already drank too much and threw parties in order to have her friends bring her the beverages that she could not legally purchase on her own. She was quite inebriated by the time we arrived. Since I was the only one with the patience and tact to talk to her, we spent the evening together as she gradually became less and less coherent. As I was leaving that night she followed me outside onto the balcony and invited me to return the next evening. There was a sudden steely soberness and a poignant pleading to her invitation that led me to accept in spite of my misgivings. She had something she wished to show me, about which she wanted to get my opinion, she said. I suppose I sensed her loneliness and unhappiness, and could not turn my back on someone in such distress.

I arrived early the next evening, hoping to fulfill my obligation and then quickly leave. She had not been drinking. She seemed quite composed and purposeful, very different from her manner the evening before. She offered me something to drink but took nothing herself. At length she said she had bought a new dress and wanted to try it on for me to see what I thought. I admit I was taken aback, but having come this far I could see no polite way to refuse. I suppose too I was becoming curious to know how all this would turn out. She went into the next room and returned with the dress, one of those filmy, gossamer gowns very lovely to look at but much too revealing and explicit for one so young. While I watched, too caught up to do anything else, she calmly disrobed until she stood before me completely nude and innocently asked if I would help slip the gown over her head.

She seduced me, my friend. And once she got started I confess I became a willing participant. I am ashamed to admit it—I was almost old enough to be her father—but it is true nevertheless. The next evening I returned, this time bringing with me drinks, and we spent the entire night making love, all our inhibitions swept away. She was a delicate and desirable creature, so young and tender and vulnerable. Yet when we made love she was mature beyond her years and possessed all the wisdom of the ages. I could not—I did not—resist her. Perhaps I would have come to my senses in time, I don't know; because without warning she ended our little affair. A short time later she took her own life.

Barbiturates and booze, my friend; who knows if it was an accident or not? I learned later, though I had no wish to know the truth I could not face, that she singled me out because I reminded her of her father, with whom she was engaged in a bitter struggle over the control of her life. At some point she confronted him—taunted him, I was told—with our affair. Then in a moment of anger and despair took those actions that cost her life.

I had not seen it coming, so I was left to wonder what the outcome could have been. I had certainly sensed she was a troubled person that first evening. But I had been only too willing to overlook that in the fleeting pleasure of the moment. The feelings exchanged between us in those few evenings together were genuine and brought both of us some respite from the troubles that led us to indulge them. In the satisfaction that my pleasure gave me, I was content to ignore that subtlety about the world that the least unhappiness signals, my friend. What subtlety is that? Irony, my friend. That nothing is ever as it appears. That unhappiness persists even in the throes of pleasure. We may ignore the irony, but we cannot escape it even if we wish to.

Shortly afterwards an unexpected encounter with a queer young man left me disturbed and uncertain and further undermined me. He approached late one night in the darkness of the dimly lighted parking lot and inquired, all very calmly and matter-of-factly, whether I knew anyone in the apartments who might be interested in a certain kind of sexual experience. He was offering his services. I will not put the proposition in the same blunt terms that he did, but I am certain you get my meaning. His question, and his calm, forthright manner caught me completely off guard and I didn't immediately know what to say. I could not begin to imagine how to respond to a question that until that moment I could not imagine ever being asked. I certainly did not suspect that the question was directed at me. I finally stammered that I knew nothing about that sort of thing, but the diffidence of my reply did not end the conversation and only served to prolong it. He was a personable, even charming, young man, with fine clean-cut looks, who seemed in genuine need of someone to talk to.

After a few minutes he no longer appeared threatening, and since I had let the initiative pass to him and didn't know how to graciously end the conversation, I ended up inviting him in for a cup of coffee. He seized upon the books littering my floor and we talked about his college studies. We had a number of literary interests in common, in particular Camus and Dostoevsky and some of the writers of twentieth century tragedy, and the conversation extended past the first cup of coffee. I laced the next few cups with brandy, then one thing led to another until finally, uninhibited, I watched, fascinated, while he performed on me the act he had in mind. Whatever pleasure I might have experienced grew out of a morbid curiosity and was superficial and fleeting, a cheap thrill really; but his own enjoyment seemed sincere and genuine, and heartfelt. Afterwards I thought the queer young man strange and sent him away. It was several weeks before I had any desire to see him again.

I was apprehensive and uncomfortable at the prospect. I felt awkward, and more than a little guilty. But, in time, it became necessary, if for no other reason than to satisfy a curiosity about the whole incident— to return to the scene of the crime, so to speak—and to put a more human, or perhaps more ordinary, face on it. But as it turned out he had no interest in seeing me, and so it ended.

These experiences left me shaken. I retreated once more to the sanctuary of my apartment and the seclusion of my reading. The words that before had been aimed directly at my inner self now seemed meant for me alone and became too painful to bear. My guilt was exposed, in all its abject misery, for the whole world to see. In a way that I had never known before, all the ills of humankind were laid directly at my door. I found in my reading more and more that depressed me, yet I was drawn to it like a moth to a flame. I had to find out each dark secret about myself, each sordid crime of which I was capable and for which I was guilty. For a while I became fascinated with Augustine and Pascal and Kierkegaard, but without finding any of the solace they professed. I discovered instead a more profound skepticism. All I found were more persuasive reasons for my own complicity and guilt. The analysis and critique of Nietzsche seemed to promise a way out, but without the forgiveness or compassion I was seeking. I was not equal to his stern demands.

Yet while there remained a glimmer of hope I determined not to give up. One day I glanced out my window and caught sight of a striking woman I had not seen before, striding along the sidewalk past my apartment. In that one brief glimpse I detected about her an indefinable something that triggered in me an immediate response. I crossed quickly to the window for a better look. She was clearly no beauty yet there was definitely something beautiful about her. She appeared matronly, with refined, dignified features, tastefully dressed and handsomely groomed. Trying to remain unobtrusive I watched as she walked by, then stepped out my door to watch her walk away. She glanced back once to find me looking at her, then glanced back a second time in an unmistakable display of interest. Only partially concealed beneath her emerging corpulence was a still pretty, vivacious face. There passed between us an animal attraction that sent a tingle of excitement racing through me. As I watched her walk away, my friend, I thought that she strode atop those too ample hips like a veritable colossus of fecundity, and I felt a desire to reap the bounty of that harvest. I was smitten.

She had recently moved into an apartment in one of the other buildings in my complex. I lost no time in learning who she was and in finding a pretext to introduce myself and invite her out to dinner. She accepted at once but insisted instead that she prepare dinner at her place. I was delighted at the prospect. I crossed her threshold that evening with eager anticipation. Like others before me I soon discovered it would not be so easy to break the bargain I had struck.

We dined in that evening—and for many evenings to come. We hardly ever ventured out. She was very solicitous and attentive to my wants and needs. That first evening we spent the night together. She was generous and accommodating in her love-making. She knew how to give pleasure unashamedly and derived genuine pleasure herself. She never refused me and expected only the same in return.

Then gradually the solicitude and attention became imposing, and confining, and then, by degrees, more forceful and demanding. Whenever I was thoughtful or quiet or moody, or whenever I stayed away for even the briefest time, she became covetous of my attention and complained that I was neglecting her or hiding something she had done to displease me. We would spend the night together and everything would be all right again, for a while. Little by little I gave up any pretense of solitude. Even when I found time to be alone, or to lose myself in my thoughts, I could not escape a nagging dread of the consequences.

I had left any hope of independence and solitude at the foot of that too ample bed, my friend. Though I did not surrender my own apartment I had practically moved in with her. Any who saw us come and go would have drawn the obvious conclusion about our relationship. Whenever I tried to suggest any change in our arrangement she became resentful and accusing. Hadn't I accepted all that she had done for me? Wouldn't anyone have interpreted my actions and my intentions toward her as a commitment to at least give this relationship a fair chance? What had she done that made me now want to change my mind? What would everyone who had seen us together these past few months think of her if I left now? Was she not good enough in bed? Could there be someone else? The accusations and the questions ran the gamut.

Against the backdrop of my present relationship I could not get out of my mind the raw tumultuous passion of that brief encounter with the enigmatic woman next door. I was puzzled by what it had meant, why it happened, and wondered whether anything approaching it could be possible again. Her accusations elicited the guilt I felt over the death of that young girl I had so willingly let seduce me. Rather than face the depression brought on by the memories of that affair, I gave in to her demands each time and took some measure of solace in her bed.

But like Odysseus trapped on the couch of the soft-braided nymph Kalypso, I wearied of my conjugal duties, afraid also to face the burden of new guilt that would descend on me at the end of this current affair. Mired in indecision and pity I did what each of us does best in such circumstances—I simply did nothing, my friend. My crippling inaction and guilt left me depressed. The depression in turn rendered me impotent. My impotence broke the only real bond between us and gave her the excuse she needed to reject me. We were both relieved at the outcome. In her mind it had all been my fault, and unavoidable, the sooner dealt with the better. I regained my independence and solitude in return for assuming the guilt that by now I had come to expect anyway—that I had even come to depend upon, my friend.

My feelings of guilt were further reinforced by the aftermath of our affair. This woman, it turns out, had a nephew who was a prominent attorney. He advised her to seek damages. Some of our love-making had been, shall we say, unorthodox, and she brought charges against me, accusing me of sexual deviancy, a kind of abuse best described by a certain biblical term. What had at the time seemed like innocent pleasure engaged in by mutual consent was made the object of an official inquiry in which my morality and my worth as a human being were under attack. I was held up to public ridicule for what I took to be perfectly normal behavior. Under that embarrassing and humiliating scrutiny I not only accepted my guilt but began to doubt my humanity as well. Finally, in the end, it was all resolved by the attorneys.

There were subsequent affairs, a number of them. Some I initiated; others I simply responded to. All of them brought me some pleasure, even brief happiness. I dare say the pleasure and happiness were mutual in most instances. But all of them were doomed at the outset by my growing, almost pathological, need to bear the burden of guilt. I would initiate failure in order to feel responsible, or more often I would simply do nothing, knowing subconsciously that failure would be the result and I could assume my rightful guilt. Several of these relationships were with women who had more than a casual interest, to whom I was likewise attracted. I know that more than one was devastated when things did not work out and we broke off our affair. Even now I have the deepest regrets about the pain I caused. In some cases I still think about what might have been.

After each of these affairs I would retreat to the solitude of my apartment and closet myself with my books, to read and fuel the oppressive obsession with my guilt that was slowly crushing the life out of me. I feared for my mental health, my friend. I knew that if I did not take some step soon to break this morbid cycle I might reach a point beyond which there would be no escape.

As my depression deepened I began to feel responsible for every single woe of the world, no matter how insignificant or trivial. Events and scenes that did not faze others reduced me to tears and plunged me to the depths of depression. The sight of an old woman standing alone in the cold waiting for a bus; a child deprived and peering longingly through a store window; grim faced people eating in stony silence; the smell of fresh mown grass; the sounds of Christmas carols. My appetite vanished, and I did not want to get out of bed. When I did, I could not function. I wished only to sit alone in the darkened silence of my room and do nothing. That of course was not possible. Not if I was to survive and maintain control. One day a voice from inside—that inner being I recognized as my one true self, I believe—told me that I must act now before it was too late.

Ah, your tears, my friend; I have upset you. I see. You have felt the same way before. Then you know. I am truly sorry for reminding you and putting you through this. But I am not in the least surprised. Far more of us than dare ever confess it have found themselves in similar straits. Considering the world we live in, and what we have made of it, it is a wonder at times that any of us maintains our equilibrium. Only those with little imagination survive unscathed. Yes, I do recall it: "Reality is only for those with no imagination." It is why we turn to so many palliatives: to sex, drugs, religion, wars, terror; to all of the various *isms* of the moment by which we try to avoid what we cannot confront about the world. Camus would have us reject any solace from the absurdity, as a negation of the world itself, and I happen to think he is right; but not everyone has the strength to revolt and strive to live always in the sunlight. And at times the darkness can be overwhelming. As Voltaire asked, and answered, "What are we to do? Let's work without theorizing; it's the only way to make life bearable. We must cultivate our garden." Look around you. I dare say everyone here this evening is at the moment living without theorizing. Whatever gets them through the night. Seemingly it is working.

What did I do, my friend? What would you expect? I confronted what most depressed me. And in trying to help a poor old woman who was ill and in desperate need and whose family had not the means to help, I took her burden upon myself, personally. She was grateful, and gracious, and she thanked me for my help and for my concern. Yet she also gently—but firmly—corrected me. Her plight was not my responsibility, she lectured me. She would not have it. It was hers alone, she said. It was what life had dealt her, what she had to show for a lifetime of struggle, "in the agony and sweat of the human spirit," as someone has described it. She would not see it all wiped out and invalidated by having anyone else take the responsibility. It was her life not mine. I could not assume what was rightfully hers, she told me. She would not agree to it, and I had no right to suggest it. She took the help I offered. She would not have, she assured me, except that she had no choice, yet she was truly thankful for my assistance. She said she hoped I would understand and not be offended.

I left there shaken. Such courage tore at my heart and left me weeping. In that first flood of emotion I still failed to grasp what she was trying to tell me. Slowly the "arrogance of my presumptions" registered. Yes, you discern correctly, my friend. No one else has ever guessed. I am thinking of Ivan Illich. Who was I to assume responsibility for the world's ills? Who had put me in charge? What reason was there to believe anyone was in charge when the evidence all pointed elsewhere? What arrogance made me demand to be in control of circumstances beyond our understanding? Not only was I being arrogant, but cowardly too. I still could not face the truth but had hidden behind the need to be in control, not just of my destiny, but in control of the fate of others. I still had not broken free from that yoke of determinism that had been my dream, a world not beyond our understanding and hence always under our control.

One should not shed tears of despair at the courage of an old woman who lectured me on my arrogance. One should weep for joy at the clarity of her truth and vision. I am still torn by the burdens and misfortunes of others, and I cannot bear to turn my back on those in need. But I no longer become depressed or insist on trying to take charge of their burdens for them. Instead I am bolstered by the unswerving courage and the undaunted spirit of the most ordinary of us in living our lives. That courageous old woman is the rule not the exception. Most people live lives of quiet desperation, someone has said. But he got it wrong, my friend. They don't, because they refuse to. They live their lives courageously, on whatever terms are granted, doing what is required of them, experiencing life *as it is*, not according to someone's *idea* of life. Given other circumstances they would undoubtedly prefer other choices. But that does not invalidate what they do, faced with the circumstances they have been dealt. No one has the right to demean all that courage, and all those lives, by becoming depressed that we cannot also be omniscient and omnipotent.

That is how I found myself in the ranks of those demonstrators I spoke of earlier, my friend. If I could not be responsible for the world's ills, then I would at least work on behalf of some great and justifiable cause. What might qualify as a sufficiently worthy cause? To save the world? Yes, but from what, my friend? Is there something that could actually threaten the world about which you or I or anyone else could do anything? If so, then perhaps it was not really a threat. I had made that mistake once, and I was not about to subject myself to the same distortion again. But let me ask you. I assume what you really mean is to save ourselves? That is a different matter entirely. The world could manage just fine without us. It has before, and it will again, in time.

Nevertheless I agree. We regard the great causes as those that combat our peril. That partially explains why they are so popular at the present moment. Public opinion holds that we face no shortage of perils, though it is hard to imagine it hasn't always seemed so, given the nature of the world and our species. Still, causes abound, and one has only to decide which among them is the most deserving at any given moment. That decision hinges on what you believe most threatens us. How can we ever decide, my friend, without first knowing the answers to all those unanswerable questions on which our existence and that of the world itself is predicated? Yes, it is a puzzle, isn't it? It is just another of those unanswerable questions that we set aside in order to get on with our lives. Ultimately we must live without theorizing.

When I decided to get involved I did not agonize over the reasons. I chose a cause that struck me as worthy and poured myself into it with all my energies. When I tired of it, I chose another. And then another, and another. Until, finally, I tired of them all.

Don't misunderstand. The causes I worked for I considered worthwhile. And I am proud of whatever contribution I might have made toward improving the lot of someone somewhere, if only for a brief span and imperfectly at that. At some point I may again choose to join the ranks of those demonstrators who had us surrounded earlier this evening.

What I tired of was the overweening arrogance of those who believe they know our true peril, to which they alone possess the answers. Under their influence what starts out as a sincere effort to do some honest good takes on a life of its own. They are spurred on and undermined by the same delusional arrogance that drove me to assume responsibility for all the world's troubles. They are driven by an obsession to be in control. If they cannot control events then they must attribute control to some higher power, or in accord with some lofty principle or moral purpose, to which they have been given privileged insight or hold some prior claim. They steadfastly deny there are no answers. In their compulsion to be in control there must be a reason for everything, and they are the ones who best understand what it is. They cannot abide the thought that things may just happen without any possibility of understanding why. The most convenient reason is that something or someone must be at fault. Circumstances are always under our control; if one pursues the chain of events far enough, someone must ultimately be responsible.

They see the world as a conspiracy of cause and effect. That view is the only one compatible with their obsession to be in control, to have an understandable reason for everything that happens. If we can but discover the cause, they believe, we can change the world so that whatever went wrong will never happen again. Whenever they are thwarted they resort to conspiracies in order to preserve the illusion of a world under control. The greater the cause the more compelling and grandiose the conspiracy, and the more diabolical those who are responsible. Everyone else becomes a victim, and victimization is worn as a badge of honor—a mark of one's status and proof of one's worthiness; vindication that our understanding of events is correct.

Yes, viewed that way we are all victims, my friend. Victimized by life itself; by the moment of conception and by the act of birth; by those who conceived us and allowed us to be born at all, and who were responsible for our upbringing. Against such an impoverished and diminished view of our existence I would hold up the courage and dignity of that old woman who upbraided me for my shallow arrogance in presuming to be responsible for what no one controls. She made me ashamed of my arrogance; theirs they wave as a banner, proclaiming that they alone have the answers. If it did not reveal such a pitiable lack of imagination that kind of arrogance would be comic. As someone has observed concerning the environmentalists, the most important thing about the environment is *them* in it. The most important thing about every great cause, my friend, is our role in it. At some point nothing else matters. Everything becomes subservient to our own aggrandizement. It becomes tiresome after a while. Even the best and most honest of intentions cannot long endure that level of hypocrisy.

I drifted from one worthy cause to another hoping to find one that was different, until I had experienced the arrogance of every great cause. And what I had once seen in myself, I saw alive in them—the cynic's truth: every noble cause is based on self-gratification. For a time I was caught up in what I was doing; I tried to believe, but it was dishonest. I kept looking for some cause that embraced humility. I could no longer abide foolish people who thought they had all the answers. They were no different from those managers I lashed out at earlier. They have the solution to every problem. When their solutions lead to other problems, well, they will have the solution to those too, and on and on, never learning from their simpleminded and ignorant foolishness. I prefer to follow someone who admits to having *no* solutions. Someone who understands that maybe there are no answers and who is still willing to act, forcefully if necessary, but in a spirit of humility and charity and compassion. Someone who does not want to lead, who came into the world "not to make it a better place, but to live in it, for better or worse."

Deliver us from the babble of those who think they know the answers, my friend. Yes, blessed are the humble, for they shall inherit the truth. As someone wryly asked, "If the universe is the answer, what the hell was the question anyway?" You see, my friend, those who think they have the answer are the most dangerous of all. For they have not even begun to understand the question.

9

Ah, you have come at last, my friend. I have been waiting anxiously for you. I was almost about to give up. I thought after the disappointment of last evening you might not return; but then it is amazing how quickly one develops a habit. As the proprietor of this establishment, I count on it.

Oh come now, you cannot deny it. It is plain to see. Do not worry yourself; I am not at all offended. You were hoping to hear of some great cause to which I had dedicated the rest of my life, some hint finally as to the secret of what life should be. All I did was disappoint you by railing at those whose arrogance makes them presume to champion great causes.

If I may speak in my defense, I would remind you I did not denigrate all causes. We must be careful to distinguish between the play and the playwright, between the playwright and the director, and between the actors on stage and off. Causes themselves were never the intended object of my ire. Far from it. Some are righteous, honorable, heroic, and frankly heartwarming. Others are essential to keep us from being trodden underfoot by the oppressors and those who would put their own interests first. Among the latter I would include those misguided champions of great causes whom I criticized so harshly. Nor did I demean the honest followers who labor in some noble undertaking against insurmountable odds. I find their courage uplifting and reassuring. It is perhaps our most admirable trait, if I had to choose but one.

No, my worthy friend, I cannot abide the insufferable conceit of those who think they possess the answers to whatever peril they happen to believe threatens us; who want to impose their paltry and meager solutions on the rest of us. I am afraid they live in a world much simpler than the one I inhabit. The only cause I wish to enlist in is life—life as it is, not as someone imagines it should be.

But come, let us not remain indoors this evening. Let us sit out on the terrace in the refreshing night air where we can look down upon that fascinating swarm of lights. The more I ponder life and the world, the more I want to be out in it, among those lights. Even I grow tired of the exalted height of this place now and then.

How quickly this desert air clears one's head, and the endless depths of the night sky restore everything to its proper perspective. Look out there, my friend: we have truly outdone ourselves. The stars are but a pale imitation of that sea of man-made lights stretching up and down the valley and out across the desert floor. They form an almost continuous glow, spreading its luminous haze from horizon to horizon. The desert air dancing in the evening zephyr causes the lights to twinkle and shimmer in rhythmic unison, like the beating heart of the universe that spawned them. From here there is no way to distinguish their beauty from that of the other natural wonders in our world. That glow which diffuses into the night sky is as natural as we are, and as magnificent as any spectacle on earth. Just not as permanent or enduring, and at this moment permanence is of little concern.

But as we draw nearer, that continuous glow breaks up and separates into individual points of light, between which there are shadows. The closer we get, the more it is the dark spaces between the lights that we notice. In those shadows, my friend, are faces. And on some of those faces are expressions of hopelessness and desperation and pain. What are we to make of all those troubled expressions amid such dazzling beauty? What answer are we to give to all those inquiring, expectant looks?

That is the most difficult question of all, my friend—the one most without any answer. And it is the one most in need of an answer. Until we answer it each of us must suffer along with all those suffering faces— or surrender our humanity. It is the question we have been pursuing: the question of life as it should be, in the face of life as it is. No matter that it is unanswerable. It demands of us a response. It is still for each of us to decide.

Like a scene in an Impressionist painting, it is in the shadows that one finds the world—and life—depicted as it really is; not in sharp, clear focus the way we would like to imagine it, but in terms of shadows that themselves have shadows which in turn have more shadows, ad infinitum. There is an infinite gradation of meaning to life, my friend. Like the infinite variety of form and shape and color I discovered in the world inside my one room apartment, or the multitude of shadows in those dark spaces between the lights. And it is in the dimmer light of those shadows that one must look hardest to find the answer we seek.

Do you see that twin row of lights in the distance, towering above and shining more brightly than those around them? Yes, those are the ones I mean. Beacons of hypocrisy, my friend. They are the lights of a sports stadium. Not just any sports arena. Those are the lights at the University, the traditional home of answers, my friend. All I know about ethics, someone once said, I learned on the football field, or something to that effect. What is done in the glare of those lights has the potential for teaching us about life, make no mistake about it. But it also has the potential for merely training us in the hypocrisy of the world. Those towering beacons should mirror the bright torch of truth that one expects to light the halls of such a venerable institution. There one expects to find the spirit of Socrates, still going about in search of answers, aware only that he does not know. Before embarking on my present mission, I too enlisted in that great cause.

I thought that perhaps a life lived as I had lived mine might lead to lessons of some use to others. I did not go to teach at the University, however, since I was not interested in teaching my chosen profession. I was not interested in *training* anyone—others could do that. I was more interested in education, and that is something very different from training. There is no dearth these days of trained ignoramuses. They are among the reasons we find ourselves in this fix, and why we cannot get out of it.

I went instead to teach the liberal arts, that noble and honorable tradition comprising the education of a truly liberated individual. Liberated from what, you ask? From illusions, my friend. From the mistaken belief that one knows something. And from the error that there is really anything more than this one simple, democratic truth to be known in the first place. It amounts to more than that. One must first embrace this simple truth and make it one's own—until it has lost its hold over us, all its power to daunt, to threaten and cower and intimidate us. Then one must learn to love it—no, not *learn* to love it, but *come* to love it—as the source of all solace and inspiration, as the wellspring of all that we aspire to. That is the only secret, my friend, the one simple truth that can liberate us. The one thing of which my life has assured me. In our ignorance is to be found the answers we seek. I am not talking about facts. Of course there are always facts; and one can know them, to be sure, but so what? Facts do not answer questions. They only raise more questions. *Beyond facts.* That is where we discover ourselves.

And that is where I wished to venture. I was at once disillusioned and disappointed. I was puzzled by the attitudes of those I encountered in the Academy. Most were not interested in education at all, but in training, and furthermore did not understand the distinction. They wanted to turn out little clones of themselves, only not as good, for that would have threatened them and heightened the chronic insecurity from which most of them suffered. Those who were more secure in their powers and professed an interest in education, too often saw teaching as the practice of proper pedagogy. Education was viewed as a problem to be solved, a puzzle to be unraveled by some better technique, some newer technology, some more appropriate curriculum, some meaningless administrative innovation. Give them all computers, or teach them all *this* way, or teach them *this thing* or *that thing*, or, most egregious of all, *manage* the situation in this fashion or that fashion, and everything will be solved, they said. Worse still, most believed they *had* the answers, that the solution lay in some answer. To suggest otherwise would have devalued what they taught and questioned their necessity and importance in the overall scheme of things. They loved to tell the story about the naked emperor but they never seemed to get the point.

What is education, besides reading and reflection? All the rest is merely training, and only so much of that is required as makes it possible to read and reflect. But read what, you are thinking? Anything and everything, my friend. Exactly *what* matters far less than just reading. To gain knowledge—treatises on science and the practical arts, and works of history. To be informed and sharpen the critical faculty of reason—essays and arguments and works of analysis and philosophy. To discover what it means to be human—novels and literature. To understand the world of which we are all part—the enduring documents of the past—the Great Books. It is not necessary to be more specific than that. Better not to get caught up in the pointless controversy over which works are the most deserving. The canon wars serve no purpose beyond acknowledging that some works are more highly esteemed than others. Read and you will be led to them in time by what you have read. But always with the realization that the answers we seek are not to be found in the pages of a book. The most one can hope for from that direction is to gather clues about how to search for the answers.

There is no problem here in need of a solution, unless it is that one—to read and reflect—and the solution to it can occur anywhere. Even then it is never solved; indeed it can never *be* solved since there is no end to it. By its nature reflection never ceases. And the kind of reflection I have in mind does not occur in the false glare of truth that illuminates the halls of Academia. That is merely the bright light of hypocrisy. Learning is more likely to occur in this school up here on the side of the mountain than in that one down there, my friend. Or on the field of that sports arena—after one has turned out the lights and sent the crowd away. We must look in the dimmer light of those shadows to find the answer we seek. Even then we will not find it, but at least we may come to better understand how to search for it.

How are we to answer then? If by now you do not know, my friend, then I have failed as Professor of the Philosophy of Life as It Is. During the past few evenings I have said it as well, and in as many ways, as I know how. There is really nothing more I can add.

There is no further need to try and explain what cannot be explained; what simply has no explanation. To explain life is a contradiction in terms, my friend. This is an existence without answers, without purpose, without design, without cause and without effect, without rhyme or reason, without justice or injustice, without perfection or imperfection. Without any *predicates* at all: it merely *is*. Like the fallacy in the ontological proof of God, existence conveys no specific predicates, no properties beyond the state of being. Nor can any predicate, no matter how shining and desirable, endow existence. The world exists, it is, and there is nothing more that we are justified in asserting.

How can one live with that realization? How could one live any other way, my friend? To have our existence determined by unfathomable predicates? That would be the worst fate of all. This way nothing is uncertain because life is without certainty or uncertainty, it merely is, that is all. That is what keeps it fresh and exciting and full of wonder: its unrelenting, undiminishable mystery. No amount of knowledge, no facts, no understanding, no science can ever remove the mystery at the core of it, no matter how much we may wish it or beguile ourselves into believing otherwise. Believe it if you wish—or if you must—but deep down, there amid the shadows in the dark spaces between the lights, you will understand it is no more than a groundless hope.

Ah, yes—our peril. The dreaded knocking at our door, like

Beethoven's three G's and an E flat. What of it, my friend? Surely by now you must realize there is no peril. There is only our existence: that which is. What you see around you is all there is, the only truth. No one has the answers to what we face, what awaits us. There are no answers because there is no question, really. Life is not a problem in need of a solution, not a question in search of an answer. The record of our existence—not some desired outcome or future prospect—is the only sense there is to be made of it.

We face no peril, my friend, only whatever will be—the truth. To think otherwise is to live in constant fear, looking always over our shoulder in hopes that we can avoid the unavoidable, know the incomprehensible, escape the inevitable. You no doubt know the passage: When I was a child, I thought like a child, I spoke like a child, I reasoned like a child; when I became a man, I gave up childish ways.

Each of us must live with the realization that there are no answers. There is only life as it is—not as it should be. We must confront that reality, courageously, without hiding behind false hopes. We cannot escape necessity, my friend. We may choose to deny it, but the world will impose it on us anyway. That is why I have done the talking. There is really nothing for the distinguished Philosopher of Life as It Should Be to add. My mission, my calling if you wish—the one great cause to which I have dedicated myself—is to profess that message nightly on this stage to this audience—all of whom have at one time been part of the cast—then send them away to act out that lesson by deciding for themselves what life should be. For it is only after confronting the reality of life as it is that we are prepared to understand what life should be.

But of course, my friend. You are right to insist upon it. We must answer; and we have answered. What cannot be answered can *always* be answered, and in many different ways. Since there is no *one* answer, there are *many* possible answers. It is for each of us to decide. There is the truth of the poet, and the truth of the physicist or the philosopher. It all depends on how we choose to view the world. We are the ones who must choose. No one can do it for us. We must decide what answers we will give to the unanswerable questions of our existence, never forgetting that no answers are ever given for us. All that we must insist on is to resist the zealot or fanatic who believes his is the only answer, for whatever misguided reason or purpose. That is to say, my friend, our answers must always be aware of all the other possible ways to answer.

Now, my friend, it is your turn. My task is finished and yours just beginning. To your credit you have stayed the course, as it were, and heard me out—or all that I care to say. I have given you one example of life as it is. It is my own, but no less general for that. All around you are other examples, each one different, yet the same in those distinctive features that characterize our existence. Now you must decide for yourself. When you have figured it out you must come back and tell me, for I will be here—eager to learn from you, as I have from all of them. More likely I will see you acting it out, the way each of your predecessors has done, the way they do nightly here on this grand stage. For you see, these are all Distinguished Chairs of the Philosophy of Life as It Should Be, each of them occupied by someone who has sat where you are sitting and heard my tale, then faced the necessity of deciding for themselves what life should be. Each is also a Chair of the Philosophy of Life as It Is, for the two are one and the same, since all that counts is what we do—not what we profess. In the final analysis there can be no distinction between life as it is and life as it should be. Our actions determine them both.

Yes, we are guided by our hopes. And by our dreams and our aspirations and our beliefs. And by whatever meaning we can manage to fashion out of our experiences and the meager facts of our existence. As I have told you, I am not advocating a philosophy of passivity, or one of resignation either. Be bold. Reach for the stars. Aspire greatly and strive greatly. Take whatever direction and follow whatever course you think you must. Use whatever tools you will. The choice—if not the outcome—is entirely up to you.

But what do I think about life as it should be? Why, I thought you might have guessed, my friend. Frankly, I do not think about it at all. I am guided only by life as it is, the only life I can live, my own, my friend. You see I believe things are pretty much as they should be. For my part I would not presume to change a thing. If so, then why am I here each evening, professing on this stage? I am here, my friend, precisely because I do believe it. And because, in spite of that, we each still must answer, we still must choose, every moment, in every action. Just because things are pretty much as they should be, doesn't mean that every answer or every choice, now or in the past, is equally acceptable or defensible. Does that mean I have contradicted myself? No, my friend, of course not. But then, that's just the point, isn't it?

READERS GUIDE

An important key to reading and understanding any work of fiction is to keep in mind two closely related questions: What is the writer doing? and How does he, or she, do it? Trying to answer these two questions as you read will generate important insights into the structure, content and meaning of the work.

These questions are especially relevant to *Parodies of the Fall*. The novel is divided into chapters, each of which is specifically structured to disclose some new aspect of the narrator's character and outlook on life.

1. Can you summarize very briefly, as you read each chapter, what new aspects it reveals about the narrator's character and his story? Done carefully, this is really the only guidance necessary to read the novel closely and critically, and understand the narrator's story.

2. In Chapter 1, the narrator contrasts *truth* and *hope*. Which, in his view, is the more important? What evidence do we find that, in spite of his somber tone, he is still at heart an optimist?

3. Can you identify examples of the stark realism that intrude on the youthful idealism of the narrator in Chapter 2, as he sets out to understand the world?

4. What becomes of his youthful quest for certainty in Chapter 3? Why does he conclude: "How much happier I am now, my friend, not ever being able to know the truth?" What do you think he means by that ironic conclusion?

5. The narrator, in Chapter 4, describes how he turned from being a

scientist to being the consummate *technician*, that mixture of *Homo sciens*, *Homo faber* and *Homo ministerium* that he refers to as the *scientist-technician*. What distinction does he draw between scientist and technician? How does he justify his new behavior as scientist-technician? Is he being sincere, or merely arrogant and self-serving?

6. He chooses to work on the bomb, but argues that, "The bomb will be used again, my friend; the dangers will be with us always. Once I realized it, I felt a great sense of relief, and I ceased to worry about it any further." What do you think he means by such a contrary conclusion? How can he justify his choice and at the same time defend his conclusion?

7. In Chapter 5, the focus of the narrative shifts from the technological to the natural world, using time as a broad measure of each. What in the narrator's consciousness replaces the mechanical timepieces and clocks by which he formerly told time? In what way(s) does his life change as a result?

8. The narrator argues that, "We can comprehend our insignificance and still be assured of our importance. The two are not contradictory; they are the same thing." Explain what he means by this ironic statement.

9. The narrator asks "Which of us finds it possible to act strictly in accordance with our convictions?" What does he mean when he asks, "Must we live a lie then? Only if we choose to deny our actions, my friend. Yet most of us will find it necessary at some point."

10. Why does the narrator simplify his life by moving into a tiny, modest—even shabby—apartment? What is he seeking? Describe his observations of his apartment, the general appearance, the shapes of things, and finally the colors. "I would sit and stare at my surroundings and regard my situation." Why might he refer to this as a work of great *deliberateness* and "a mental work of monumental proportions?"

11. The narrator concludes that, "The artist alone does not get to make art, my friend. The artist must have his audience. Only together can they make art."

Apply that meaning to the pictures on the wall of his apartment. How do you think the narrator would answer his own question, "Was it I, or the painter who did not even bother to sign them, that made the pictures on my wall into art...""?

12. What do you think the narrator means by the statement, "Life is the continual unfolding of art; art is the constant expression of life."?

13. Explain the narrator's statement that, "Materialism has not caused the collapse of society, my friend; it is what sustains us and keeps it going." What, in his view, is the central motivating fantasy of our society that explains capitalism?

14. What does the narrator hope to accomplish by his frenzied schedule of reading? Why does his plan fail? What is accomplished?

15. For what purpose in his story do you think the narrator discloses to the listener his abortive affairs? What was the eventual outcome of these affairs? And how do they influence the direction of the narrator's story?

16. What does the narrator mean by, "...the cynic's truth: every noble cause is based on self-gratification?" What is the nature of his criticism?

17. What does the narrator mean when he says, "You see, my friend, those who think they have the answer are the most dangerous of all. For they have not even begun to understand the question?" Who exactly is he criticizing by this statement?

18. What do you think the narrator means when he says, "In our ignorance is to be found the answers we seek?" Who do you think is he adopting as the model of inquiry by this statement?

19. Explain how the narrator's concluding remark can serve as the point of the story?